Randy,

God Bless You.

Jim Bakker
1 Pe 5:7

MAJOR LEAGUE DAD

Randy -
I am so thankful for
our friendship. May God be
the witness to our growth
as we lead our families to
eternity, I love + appreciate
you.

Randy -
I am so thankful for
our friendship. May we be

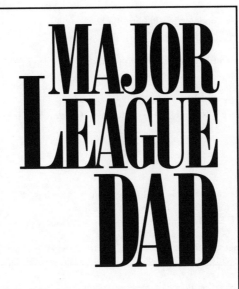

MAJOR LEAGUE DAD

TIM & CHRISTINE BURKE

WITH GREGG LEWIS

PUBLISHING

Colorado Springs, CO

Library of Congress Cataloging-in-Publication Data

Burke, Tim, 1959-
    Major league dad / Tim and Christine Burke with Gregg Lewis.
        p.   cm.
    ISBN 1-56179-212-8
    1. Burke, Tim, 1959-   2. Baseball players—United States—Biography.   3. Father
and child.   I. Burke, Christine, 1961-   II. Lewis, Gregg A.   III. Title
GV865.A1B865   1994
796.357'092—dc20
[B]   94-3069
                                                                                                        CIP

Published by Focus on the Family Publishing, Colorado Springs, CO 80995.

Distributed in the U.S.A. and Canada by Word Books, Dallas, Texas.

Unless otherwise noted, Scripture quotations are from the Holy Bible, New International
Version, copyright © 1973, 1978, 1984 by the International Bible Society.

Editor: Larry K. Weeden
Front cover illustration: John Ward
Back cover photo: Susie Klenk

Printed in the United States of America
94 95 96 97 98/10 9 8 7 6 5 4 3 2

*We passionately dedicate this book to our precious children.
Without you, we would never have known what it was like to
be Mommy and Daddy. Thank you, Ryan, Stephanie, Nicole,
Wayne, and the rest yet to come home.*

Contents

FOREWORD

Sometime during baseball season in 1988, I was introduced to Tim Burke. Craig Reynolds, a mutual friend who played for the Houston Astros, called me one afternoon, mentioned that the Montreal Expos were in town, and said that some of them were familiar with my music and would like to meet. After the game, we enjoyed a late dinner and a good time of fellowship. In this small group of new friends was a tall, soft-spoken guy named Tim Burke.

I'd seen Tim on the pitching mound and couldn't believe it was the same person. On the field, he was intense. After striking out a hitter, he would pace around the mound, pounding his glove hand with his fist. Mercy wasn't part of his plan when facing an opposing hitter. But here was a man in whom I sensed great mercy, great tenderness, and a peaceful but all-consuming love for the Lord.

I sat somewhat in awe that night. After all, these guys were in the big leagues! I've discovered since that a lot of ballplayers dream of being musicians, and vice versa. Tim and I had an immediate appreciation for one another and a wonderful common bond in our devotion to our Lord and to our families.

One of the ways I could tell, from that first meeting, that this was going to be a special friendship was that we were mutually, intensely interested in each other's lives. Some conversations are little more than battles over who gets to do most of the talking. With Tim and me, that was not and never has been the case. There were lots of questions from one to the other, lots of listening, and plenty of genuine hearing! I knew that Tim and I would be great friends and brothers.

God cemented our devotion as friends through the coming months and years. We would be in each other's paths at the most interesting times—good times and bad, but doubtless times that could only have been ordained and orchestrated by the Lord.

I remember, for instance, when Nicole was adopted into the Burke household. At only ten months old, she was in desperate need of open-heart surgery. Yes, Tim and Christine were aware of her need before she was brought to America from Korea. I was in Montreal with the Burkes for the surgery. I didn't really know why I was compelled to go to Canada at the time. But God was teaching me how to be a friend, and that's what friends do. Tim met me at the airport, and from there we were *supposed* to go to Olympic Stadium, where he was *supposed* to play a ballgame. Nicole's surgery was scheduled for the very next day.

The look on Tim's face when we met told me that something was wrong. He was in obvious emotional pain. My first thought was that perhaps something had gone wrong with Nicole, that the surgery would be too late. "You'll never guess what happened today," he said. "I've been traded to the Mets! The Mets!" he almost yelled.

I knew then why the Lord had written me in on this little chapter of their lives. Tim and Christine were as despondent as I'd ever seen them. The timing just didn't make sense. I knew that my job was to try to point out the good side of going to play for the New York Mets. It was a tall order! I don't remember much of what was said, but I felt secure in the knowledge that it was God speaking. And I remember a few laughs coming from the front seat . . . some trust being reestablished and God's bigger view beginning to come into focus.

I suppose there are many levels of friendship. But those that go the deepest and last the longest endure some tension, more than a few questions, seasons of distance, quiet, good times, and some tears. I've been blessed to share all of those experiences with Tim and his family. To say I've been inspired by the bigness of their hearts would be a tremendous understatement. A song on my album "A Beautiful Place" called "A Place for You" was written for and about them. Their love for their children who have come from so many different parts of the world is a wonderful parallel to the love God has for us all. Aren't we all orphans, homeless, looking for a place to be loved . . . looking for a home? While Tim and Christine continue to open their hearts and lives to more needy children, I'm always reminded of the boundless love and the open arms of our heavenly Father.

From personal experience, Tim and Christine Burke know words like *despair* and *loneliness*. They know what it means to live apart from the grace and mercy of our Lord. Today, however, the heart of the indwelling Christ is easy to see in them. I know that everyone who reads this book will be encouraged and reminded of the long reach of the loving arms of God, and of the fact that God still changes hearts for more than just survival or a mundane existence. Hearts put into His hands are constantly molded into works of art bringing honor and glory to Him. That's what I see in my friends Tim and Christine Burke. I think you'll see it, too.

Wayne Watson
February 1994

CHAPTER ONE

The Final Out

Tim

FEBRUARY 27, 1993. PLANT CITY, FLORIDA.

The locker room at the Cincinnati Reds training camp seemed quieter than usual that Saturday morning. Or maybe I just subconsciously shut out all the usual commotion in order to keep up with my own racing thoughts and complete the task at hand.

As I pulled three pairs of size 11 spikes from the bottom of my locker and stashed them in my equipment bag, I remember thinking, *I'm not going to be needing these anymore.* I fought the urge to slide my hand into my glove and feel its familiar leather shape. *No sense prolonging this ordeal.* I tossed my glove into the bag.

My workout clothes went in on top of that. Sweat pants. A couple of pairs of shorts. Then the red, long-sleeved t-shirts I wore beneath my uniform. Finally, a change of street clothes.

Still hanging in my locker was my uniform, with "Cincinnati" emblazoned across the front and "Burke" stitched above the number 47 on the back. As I pulled the hangers out of the locker, I was saddened by the realization, *I'll never wear this uniform in a game.* It seemed ironic after the excitement my wife, Christine, and I had felt when I signed my free-agent contract with the Reds a little more than three months earlier.

Walking across the locker room to turn in my uniform to the equipment manager, I couldn't help but think about the other major-league uniforms I had worn during my career. For six and a half years, I proudly wore the red, white, and blue of the Montreal Expos. Then I played parts of two seasons as a New York Met, and I spent the last part of the 1992 season wearing New York Yankee pinstripes.

When I returned to my locker a minute later, the Reds' public relations director was waiting for me. "We didn't have time to set up a formal press conference," he said. "But some reporters want to talk to you."

"Okay," I replied. "When I'm finished here, I'll see them on my way out."

As I collected the last of my personal things, a couple of my new teammates strolled over to my locker. "We just heard," they said. "Is it true? You're retiring today?"

I nodded—and wondered how, in a few short words, I could even begin to answer their implied question: *Why?*

They knew, as everyone on the team knew, that Christine and I had adopted three special-needs children from overseas. We were expecting our fourth, a little Vietnamese boy with a club foot, in a matter of weeks. So I simply said, "I've decided my wife and family need me a lot worse than baseball does right now."

That was it in a nutshell. But what I didn't try to explain was the agony I had been through the last few days as I wrestled with this decision; the traumatic family events over the past few years that led up to this point; and the confusing mix of emotions churning inside me for the half hour since I walked into Manager Tony Perez's office and said, "I've decided to retire today."

Relief—that the decision was finally made.

Impatience—to be out of there.

Excitement—about beginning a whole new phase in my life.

Uncertainty, maybe even *fear*—thinking about all the future unknowns.

Confidence—that I had made the right decision.

Yet an almost overwhelming sense of *sadness*—as the implications of my decision began to sink in.

Slinging the strap of my equipment bag over my shoulder and heading for the door, I was struck by the thought, *This is the last time I'll ever be in a major-league locker room and feel like I belong here.* I had walked into the Reds' complex that morning as part of a very special fraternity, a small baseball brotherhood that ties together everyone—from superstars to rookie utility men—who wears a major-league uniform. For eight years, I had the privilege and satisfaction of knowing, "I'm a big leaguer."

No more! Walking out through the locker-room door, I realized how suddenly and totally my life had changed. *Just like that, I'm an "ex-major-league ballplayer" now.*

Six or eight reporters surrounded me the instant I left the locker room. They were newspaper guys mostly, along with some radio reporters; no television crews would be around that early on a Saturday morning. I leaned back against the nearest wall and began answering their questions.

"Why are you retiring?"

I explained that my family needed me worse than the Reds did. "Baseball is going to do just fine without me," I said. "It's not going to miss a beat. But I'm the only father my children have. I'm the only husband my wife has. And they need me a lot more than baseball does."

"How did you feel physically this spring? Did that affect your decision?"

"No," I said. "I feel great." I was throwing better than I had in years. I knew I could still get batters out and help my team win games.

"What do you think you'll miss the most?"

I felt a sudden tightness in my chest transform itself into a big lump and begin working its way into my throat. I took a deep breath. "The guys," I said. "I'll miss all the friends I've made in baseball . . ."

I paused, swallowed hard, and shifted the subject: ". . . and the competition. I'll miss the intensity of personal confrontation between pitcher and batter every time a new hitter steps into the box against me. I don't know of anywhere else you can ever find that level of pure, one-on-one competition."

"Any chance of a comeback?"

I smiled and shook my head. "No." I knew my decision was final.

The reporters had a few more questions about my family and future plans. I tried to answer them all. But the moment they stopped asking, I began walking—through the outer doors and toward the players' restricted parking lot.

All morning, I had fought to keep my emotions in check. It wasn't until I tossed my bag in the trunk of my car and slid in behind the steering wheel that I allowed myself to really feel the pain and the loss. The lump in my throat welled higher and higher, and my tear ducts began to pump. I put on my sunglasses to cover my grief.

The security guard waved as I pulled slowly through the players' gate for the last time thinking, *I'm heading into the real world now.*

As much as I tried to focus on the road and the future ahead, I couldn't help looking back with an overwhelming sense of grief and loss. I felt as if a part of me had been voluntarily amputated or a good friend had died and left me all alone.

The baseball record books had closed for Tim Burke. From 1985 through 1992, I pitched in 498 major-league games, with 49 wins, 33 losses, 102 saves, 444 strikeouts, and a lifetime ERA (earned run average—the number of earned runs a pitcher allows per nine innings pitched) of 2.72. Those few statistics summed up my entire career—a wonderful, eight-year-long dream come true; an adventure that was now over.

As that sad truth sank in, I realized no one I had talked to all morning had really understood what I was doing and why. When I told Tony Perez I was retiring, he was understanding, but he didn't really *understand*. Neither did my teammates or the reporters.

I knew what they were thinking, because I had the same thoughts myself: *What am I doing walking away from the game that has been my dream since I was a boy? How can I give up the only career I've known or prepared for—not to mention a new, one-year, $625,000 contract and the acclaim that goes with being a major-league pitcher—at the age of 34?*

But the answer to those questions is really the end of the story—a story I will tell in the rest of this book with the help of my wife. What has happened in our family, our marriage, and our lives is every bit as much her story as it is mine.

CHAPTER TWO

Hard Childhoods

Christine

LIKE TIM, I LOVED SPORTS. THEY WERE A GREAT SOURCE OF FUN and acceptance in my youth. I was involved in everything from badminton to track. I thrived on competition, and I knew how to win. But all of that changed forever one day, when I encountered an opponent I couldn't beat.

Nothing in the 14 years of my life had prepared me for the panicked, suffocating sensation of waking up in a hospital and realizing a respirator was breathing for me. And if that didn't make me feel helpless enough, my arms and hands were strapped down to keep me from thrashing around and jerking loose any of the tubes sticking out of my side and neck.

The slightest movement of my head sent searing pain shooting from the base of my skull to the tips of my toes, so I concentrated on staying perfectly still. But out of the corner of my eye, through the window of the intensive care unit (ICU), I could see Mom talking to a man. When I recognized him as the minister of the church I occasionally attended, I felt a surge of anger deep inside. If he'd come to talk to me about God, I didn't want to hear it.

The minister entered my room a few minutes later—but no one untied my hands. All I could do to convey my hostility was to refuse to even look at him. He prayed for me, and still I never acknowledged his presence. Eventually he left.

I guess I wasn't so angry at the minister—I was angry at God. *How could He let this happen?* I wanted to know. If He really was a God of love and mercy as everyone told me, how could He allow a senseless accident that killed one teenager, seriously injured four others, and left me with a broken neck that would change my life forever? I believed that if God really loved me, my entire life would have been different from the start.

As I lay motionless in that hospital bed, I thought about how my father had walked out on my mother three months before I was born, leaving her as the only parent for my three-year-old sister, Susie, my one-year-old brother, Bill, and me.

Mom had it rough. During much of my childhood, she worked two jobs—as an office worker/secretary during the day, then doing a variety of things at night. She would leave us early every morning, before we went to school, and some days we wouldn't see her again until late at night. Then she would return home to tackle housework and laundry and try to catch up on what had happened in our lives that day.

In my earliest memories, I picture Mother always looking tired. As a little girl, I watched her drag home at night and felt terribly sad that she had to work so hard to take care of us all.

Yet no matter how hard Mom worked, we always struggled financially. The year I turned two, my sister went without shoes all summer because there were more pressing family needs. I also remember the simple generosity of our landlords who felt sorry for Mom and occasionally gave each of us kids some candy or inexpensive toy we couldn't afford. Because I saw how much Mom appreciated those gifts and I enjoyed those kinds of surprises, I vowed to myself, *One day, if I ever have the money, I'm going to make people happy by giving unexpected gifts.*

When my father left, in effect he robbed me of both my parents, because with three small children to support, Mom had to be gone all day at work. In what became a vicious, inescapable cycle, Mom worked herself to exhaustion trying to meet our basic physical needs.

Yet Susie, Bill, and I so desperately wanted Mom's attention that we drove off one baby-sitter after another. We even lied to Mom about a couple of them so she wouldn't want to use them again.

By the time I turned seven, I was cared for after school most days by my ten-year-old sister, Susie. Though she was a child herself, there was no one else. Bill and I also begged Mom to give her the responsibility so we wouldn't have to have another baby-sitter. That meant no responsible adult knew what was going on in our home when my mother was gone. And because no one was there to protect me, things happened that shouldn't have.

The first affirmation that truly made me feel good about myself came from sports. I started playing organized softball at the age of ten in a recreation program at a park near our home, making the all-star team every year until I was 14. And from my earliest days in grade school, I was fast enough to compete in Omaha, Nebraska's, Junior Olympics program.

When she could, Mom came to watch me compete. But soon I became more concerned about the approval of my peers. I made friends playing sports. And they not only accepted me, but they really liked me, because I was a good athlete. A school guidance counselor called Mom to ask about getting me started in a special conditioning and training program for promising young athletes.

Then, just two weeks later, on an October evening in 1975, my life changed forever.

I had gone to our junior-high-school football game with a group of friends, and afterward we went out for pizza. Then we called home for rides as we always did. But for the first time, none of our parents were home. (I found out later that Mom had stepped out into the yard to cut a rose, heard the phone ring, and ran back inside, reaching the phone just after I hung up.)

So five of us girls, plus one girl's boyfriend, decided to walk a few blocks to the boy's house. We had gone only a short way when a couple of older teenage guys one of my friends knew drove up alongside us and asked, "Want a ride?"

We piled into the car, laughing about our good luck. But then, only six blocks down the street, a speeding vehicle swerved across the center line and slammed into us head-on, killing our driver and critically injuring four others of us in the car.

I had been in the front seat, not wearing a seat belt. The force of the collision drove me straight up, ramming my head into the roof, then hurled my body against the dashboard. I regained partial consciousness in the emergency room, with a uniformed policeman and my mother standing over me. "What happened?" I asked. "Where am I?"

Internal hemorrhaging made me look pregnant. And when the initial shock began to wear off, I felt as if someone had snapped shut a steel bear trap on the back of my neck. As I lay on a gurney outside the x-ray room, the pain grew so excruciating that I screamed, "Let go of my neck! Don't touch me!" But no one was touching me. And no one could loosen the trap I felt.

My mom gave me the bad news. "Honey," she said when the x-ray report came back, "the doctors say your neck is broken, but your spinal cord is intact. To make sure the vertebrae don't separate any farther and damage your spinal cord, they're going to have to put you in a special body brace to hold your head, chin, and back perfectly still."

A short time later, a nurse arrived with my brace. It looked like a medieval torture device. First, the nurse pulled a strap over each of my shoulders and fastened it to another part of the contraption cinched tight around my torso. Then she strapped my chin to a stiff piece of metal that was fixed to the chest portion of the brace. To that she attached a halo that held my head in place.

With each step of the process, I felt as if a piece of me died inside. The nurse was my jailer and the brace my private isolation cell. I tried to look away so the nurse wouldn't see the tears in my eyes, but I couldn't turn away at all.

She noticed, and she put her arm around me, patted my shoulder, gave me a little hug, and said, "I know how you feel."

The power of my anger startled me as I bitterly replied, "You have no idea how I feel!"

The plan was to keep me in the body brace while my multiple internal injuries healed. Then, when I was strong enough, the doctors would operate to permanently fuse two vertebrae in my neck.

After a month, the doctors sent me home in the body brace. But my broken rib and other injuries continued to take their toll. Four weeks later, after I lost 20 pounds and began to struggle for each breath, I was rushed back to the hospital with a collapsed lung. Doctors made a small incision and inserted two chest tubes to drain off fluid that had collected around the lung. Three days later, surgeons opened me up to remove blood clots from the lung.

It was after my third lung surgery in a week that I awoke on the respirator and saw the minister outside my ICU room. By then the doctor was so concerned about my condition that he told Mom, "If Christine loses the will to live, she'll die."

If I had known it would be that easy, I might have done it. I know I wanted to die badly enough.

I couldn't talk while I was on the respirator. But after making me promise not to pull out any of the tubes, Mom temporarily loosened one of my arms. I managed to scribble out a crude good-bye note saying, "I love Mom. Susie. Bill. And Benji." (Benji was more than just my dog. He was my best friend, the most reliable source of available and unconditional love in my entire life.)

Mom told me later that after she read the note and saw the empty look in my eyes, she knew I was giving up. And she began to cry. I fell asleep that night expecting to die and not caring if I did.

I remember the surprise I felt the next morning when I opened my eyes and realized, *I'm still alive!* Mom was there, smiling and promising, "Honey, the doctor says he's coming a little later this morning to remove the respirator. You'll be able to breathe on your own again."

The next day, I awakened to see Mom again. This time, she was pointing toward the window of my first-floor room. Outside, romping in a deep, new snow, were my brother, Bill, and my little dog, Benji, dressed in a bright red sweater. When I laughed at them stumbling and rolling together in the snow, Mom went to the window and motioned them over. When Bill lifted Benji in his arms, pressed his nose to my window, and waved one of his little paws, I began to cry. I so wanted to hug my little dog again.

Mom smiled, knowing that Bill and Benji had done for my spirits just what she had hoped. Slowly, I began wanting to live again.

A few months later, I underwent a cervical fusion, then returned to school soon afterward in a body cast. I wore the cast all the way up to three days before the drill-team tryouts. To my surprise, I made the team. I reasoned that if I could no longer play sports, I could at least perform at halftime. But even that proved impossibly painful, and I had to quit the squad.

Over the next couple of years of operations and rehabilitation, I slowly accepted my doctors' prognosis. They said I would have to live differently from now on. I would need to learn my limits. And I could expect to live the rest of my life with severe and chronic pain.

The limits were terribly frustrating. I dulled the pain with a steady dose of prescription painkillers until I overheard two girls chuckling over my yearbook photo. "Look at those eyes!" the first one exclaimed.

"Christine sure was drugged up that day," the second said with a laugh.

I was so mortified that I flushed every pill down the toilet. *I don't need your help anymore,* I thought. *I don't need Mom's help. Or Susie's. Or Bill's. And I certainly don't need God's help. I can handle this myself.*

At the same time I determined to be completely self-sufficient, I still desperately craved others' affirmation and approval. So I devised an all-purpose strategy that achieved both goals. For the remainder of my high-school years, I masked my physical and emotional pain by putting on a confident, cheerful, outgoing facade. And it worked. I was the only one who knew it was just an act. My classmates actually voted me "Most Popular" without ever suspecting the hurt and hypocrisy I harbored in my soul.

I never again saw the minister who visited me in the hospital, because I no longer had any interest in church. If you had asked me at the time, I would have said I still believed in God. I think I probably even believed He was a God of love.

I just concluded that, for some reason, God didn't love me.

Tim

LIKE CHRISTINE, I GREW UP WITH FAMILY TRAUMA.

I was five years old the night my mother woke my sister, Terri, and me to say, "Something terrible has happened. Dick's been in an accident." I didn't understand all that meant, but I could tell it was serious because Mom seemed so frantic.

My brother, Dick, 13 years older than me, was my personal

hero. He had played ball with me since I was a toddler. By the time I was three or four, he was telling my parents and anyone else who would listen, "Tim's going to be a professional ballplayer someday. He's a natural athlete."

According to police reports, the single-car accident occurred when Dick lost control of his car on a winding, rain-slick road. The emergency room doctors never revived him, and Dick died that night.

The next day, a steady stream of people, many of them crying, came by the house to try to console my parents. I saw an Omaha television station report Dick's death. And at the funeral a couple of days later, I walked up to Dick's casket to slip a lucky penny into his jacket pocket. When I felt his hard, lifeless body, I knew my big brother was gone forever.

But his faith in me wasn't. When I began to play Little League baseball at the age of eight, Mom would tell me what Dick used to say when he'd pitch to me and play catch in our backyard: "Someday you're going to be a big-league baseball player, Tim."

Now Terri was the one who played catch with me in the yard. Dad would come to my games when he could, but during my earliest years in baseball, his traveling sales job took him away from home a lot. So Mom came to every one of my games, screaming and cheering louder than any other parent in the stands. The older I got and the more success I had on the baseball field, the more Mom seemed to believe it when she told me I would play in the major leagues some day.

When I was nine, Mom went into the hospital for an operation to remove a lump from her breast. My dad and my sister, who was 16 years old then, had obviously been crying when they came to my friend's house where I was staying that evening to tell me, "Mom has cancer. The doctors had to remove her breast. And she's very sick."

I knew what cancer was. Dad and Terri didn't have to explain. After they went back to the hospital that night, I remember lying in my sleeping bag on the floor beside my friend's bed. Alone in the darkness, with only a sliver of light shining in under the closed bedroom door, as I listened to the rhythmic breathing of my sleeping friend, I began to cry.

Despite going to church regularly, I didn't talk to God much. But I remember the questions I hurled at Him that night. "Why?" I wanted to know. "Why does my mom have to get cancer? First my brother. Now this. Why?"

My anger, sadness, and pain seemed more than a nine-year-old heart could bear. So sometime during that long, dark, sleepless night, my subconscious made the decision, *I'm not going to be hurt anymore!* In emotional self-defense, I began closing down the feeling valves deep in the recesses of my being.

For seven agonizing years, Mom fought a valiant but ultimately futile battle against her cancer. She tried to live as normal a life as she could the first few years and any time the cancer went into remission. And she continued to cheer at my games as long as she could manage to sit in the stands.

But the cancer slowly, relentlessly ran its course. Mom never cried or complained in front of me. Neither did my dad or Terri. I think there was an unspoken conspiracy to be strong for my sake. And because no one else in my family exposed any pain, it made it easier for me to keep mine bottled up inside.

My primary strategy for dealing with my mom's cancer and my own painful feelings was to be home as little as possible. I made a deliberate effort to finish any homework at school so that when I got home every afternoon, I was free to hop on my bike and ride around the neighborhood or head to a friend's house until suppertime. After we ate, I would leave again until bedtime. If I didn't have to be home and could find enough distractions, I could go for hours without having to think, *My mom is dying.*

Baseball also helped. More than a mere distraction, athletic competition was the safety valve that allowed me to release my emotional pressure. The baseball diamond was the one place I could allow myself to let go, to express, to feel any real range of emotion. I could celebrate success without feeling guilty. I could channel my frustration into competitive intensity without worrying about my hidden anger hurting those around me. I could anguish over a loss without having to pretend I was strong.

The lower Mom sank, the tighter I closed my emotional valves. The last couple of years, it hurt so deeply to watch her lose her hair, turn yellow, and slowly wither away that I spent more and more time apart from the family. But as much as I wanted to, I couldn't play baseball 24 hours a day.

I remember many times waking up in the middle of the night and going into the kitchen for a drink of water. Mom would be huddled in a chair in our darkened living room, unable to sleep for the pain. I'd act as if I didn't see her and go back to bed without saying anything to her because I just couldn't acknowledge her suffering. In fact, she endured so much the last couple of years that I began to look forward to her death. At least death would bring an end to her pain.

I was 16 when she finally died at the age of 54. Her funeral seemed strangely anticlimactic. Her pain was over. But mine was buried so deep inside that I don't remember even crying.

Dad had given up his sales job and gone into business in Omaha so he could be home more during Mom's illness. He began coming to all my games, and he took me with him on trips to visit different major-league ballparks and see big-league games. Yet, despite the interest and faith my entire family showed in my athletic potential, I don't remember ever seriously thinking as so many boys do, *Some day I'm going to play in the big leagues.* Not that I didn't want to. The idea just seemed so far beyond my wildest dreams that I didn't allow myself to consider it seriously.

Even after I made the varsity baseball team as a sophomore and built a reputation as a high-school pitcher, I wasn't convinced I could ever play college ball. But then, during my senior year, I began receiving letters of interest from a number of schools.

Though my continued athletic success eventually enabled me to overcome my lack of confidence on the baseball field, my personal life was another story. I was an emotionally reserved, quiet, and painfully shy teenager. The only sure cure I found for that plague was drinking. I was 14 the first time I raided a stash of beer in our basement refrigerator. I loved the taste so much, I downed a six-pack before I threw up and stumbled into bed. I felt so sick the next morning that I vowed never to drink again. But when the opportunity arose months later, the beer tasted better than it had the first time. And I didn't get a hangover.

From time to time throughout high school, I drank with my friends when we could find an older guy to buy us a supply of beer. But the real drinking began after I enrolled at the University of Nebraska on a baseball scholarship.

I quickly learned I could drink more than my friends without getting sick, and I took pride in that discovery. I also learned that drinking loosened me up. Once I got a few beers in me, my natural shyness disappeared. I was more articulate, more confident, more outgoing. I could talk to girls. It was as if I became a whole new person when I was drunk—and I liked it.

While I majored in accounting and business at Nebraska, my real focus was baseball—and beer. But my heavy drinking didn't keep me from earning All-Big Eight Conference honors my sophomore and junior seasons. I left school after my junior year to sign my first professional baseball contract when the Pittsburgh Pirates selected me in the second round of the 1980 amateur draft.

The Pirates assigned me to a minor-league team in the rookie league. But when I developed tendinitis and couldn't pitch, they sent me home to sit out the remainder of the 1980 season. I saw that as a small setback. I knew I'd pitch again, and I still had a few thousand dollars of bonus money left to spend. My future seemed bright. At the age of 21, I was already a professional baseball player. That much of my brother's prediction had come true.

CHAPTER THREE

Love at
First Sight?

Tim

I'LL NEVER FORGET THE NIGHT I MET CHRISTINE.

One Saturday afternoon in the fall of 1980, I drove from Omaha down to Lincoln to visit some college teammates I hadn't seen since turning pro at the beginning of the summer. After a few hours of catching up and reminiscing on campus, my friend Mike and I went to one of our favorite bars for the evening.

For some reason, instead of getting drunk as I often did when I was out with the guys, I took it pretty easy that night. I was busy watching a cute girl I had seen come into the bar early in the evening. She looked vaguely familiar, and I kept trying to place her. *I know I've seen her before . . . but where?*

Christine

MY FRIEND SALLY HAD TALKED ME INTO DRIVING FROM OMAHA TO Lincoln because she wanted to visit another friend at the University of Nebraska. Since I had no better plans for the weekend, I agreed to go. That's how I ended up spending Saturday night sitting in a bar and talking.

Sally's friend went her own way that evening, so just the two of us were at our table when Sally said, "Don't look now, but I think that guy over there is staring at you."

I turned and noticed a nice-looking guy at a table across the way. "I don't think so," I told her. But after that, whenever I glanced toward him, he was always looking our way.

Sally noticed, too. "I told you he's looking at you."

"Stop it. He is not."

"I think maybe he likes you. He is kind of cute. Why don't you go talk to him?"

I had just broken up with a guy and wasn't the least bit interested in striking up a conversation with some staring stranger in a bar. I had already turned down a couple invitations to dance and didn't feel very sociable. But as the night wore on, I kept enough of an eye on this guy across the smoke-filled bar to decide he did, indeed, seem interested in me. He looked like a nice guy. He had an unusual smile—a smile I thought I had seen somewhere before.

Tim

I TRIED TO WORK UP MY NERVE TO TALK TO HER ALL EVENING, BUT that just wasn't my style. I was still basically very shy unless I was under the influence.

Five minutes before closing time, I decided I had to do it. If she walked out of the bar, I might never see her again. *Okay,* I told myself, *you have nothing to lose.*

As I walked across the room, I kept bumping into people I knew. Each time an acquaintance stopped me, I looked up to make sure *she* was still there. *What am I going to say? I'll ask her to dance . . . but I don't dance! What am I doing?*

By the time I finally made it to her table, the house lights had come up. Closing time. *At least I won't have to dance.*

"Uh, I know this sounds strange," I said, "but haven't I seen you somewhere before?" As an opening line, it did sound lame, so I hurried on. "You really do look familiar."

At least she didn't tell me to get lost. I introduced myself. She told me her name was Christine Atkinson. I figured she was a university student, but she said she was just visiting from Omaha. I told her I was from Omaha, too, and we began comparing notes as bouncers ushered people toward the doors.

"Everybody out. Closing time," they said.

At that point, I went from nervous to desperate. I knew I

wanted to see her again, and I didn't want to lose the chance.

Her friend Sally quickly assured me, "We can talk outside. We're in no hurry."

Once we got outdoors, Christine began shivering, so I slipped my Pittsburgh Pirates jacket over her shoulders.

"What's this?" Christine asked, noting the Pirate logo.

"Well," I told her, "I play minor-league baseball for the Pirates organization."

"Oh," she responded, obviously uncertain what I meant.

I didn't want to have to explain, so I asked her what kind of work she did. She said she was between jobs and working only part-time. And somehow, in those first few minutes of conversation, we realized we had, indeed, crossed paths just the week before.

I had been driving past an Omaha employment agency where my sister worked when I made a spur-of-the-moment decision to stop and say hello to some of the people working there. While I was chatting with the receptionist, Christine had been sitting on a nearby couch, waiting for an appointment. I noticed her at the time, and when her name was finally called and a secretary escorted her in for her interview, I watched her go and joked to the receptionist, "Hey, I might be interested in a job if I could work with her."

Christine
♥♥♥♥♥

TIM'S OPENING LINE DID SOUND CORNY, BUT IN A SINCERE SORT OF way. He seemed familiar to me, too. I don't remember how we pinned down our encounter at the employment agency so quickly, but when we did, I definitely remembered him. I had watched him talking to the receptionist and had noticed his smile. But we hadn't talked at the time, and I didn't think about it again until we finally met in the bar, more than a week later, in another town an hour's drive from where we first saw each other.

While Tim immediately struck me as a pleasant, polite guy, I wasn't going to let myself get too interested in a stranger who approached me in a bar at closing time. Yet, when he asked if maybe we could get together someplace in Omaha, I said, "I guess."

"You know a place called the Penthouse Lounge?" he asked.

I knew it too well! It was where I had just broken up with my old boyfriend, who went there a lot. "Well . . . uh . . ."

Tim took my hesitation as a sign that I wasn't interested.

"I'm sorry," he said. "You probably have a boyfriend."

"Uh, no," I assured him. "It's not that." But I didn't want to tell him the real reason. "Maybe I could meet you someplace else sometime."

"Okay," he said, "I have to leave and drop off my friend at a party. It will just take a few minutes." Then he caught me completely by surprise by saying, "I know an all-night restaurant near here. Can I take you and your friend out for breakfast?"

"Well, . . . I don't know . . . " I was thinking, *I don't know anything about this guy. He seems nice enough.* I said, "I don't think it's such a good idea . . ."

"Sounds great!" Sally blurted out. "Christine and I don't have any other plans."

"It's awfully late . . ." I tried to protest.

But Sally, warming up to her matchmaker role, was already getting directions to the restaurant and promising Tim, "We'll meet you there shortly."

I was half relieved a few minutes later when we couldn't find the place. We drove up and down the street Tim told us about, but we didn't see an open restaurant. "Let's just forget it," I said. "It's the middle of the night. We don't know anything about this guy anyway."

Sally reluctantly gave up, and we drove back to her friend's apartment to go to bed. We had just walked in the door when the phone rang. "Answer it," Sally said. "Maybe it's him."

"But how . . ."

She shrugged. "Before we left the bar, I gave him the phone number, just in case he wanted to call you," she said. I couldn't believe she had done that.

Sure enough, it was Tim. "Did you change your mind about breakfast?" he asked. I apologized and told him we couldn't find the restaurant. He said he knew another spot closer to the apartment and asked if we would meet him there. "I don't know . . .

it's so late . . ." I said, only to be interrupted again by Sally, who was listening on an extension. She said she knew right where the second place was and that we would meet Tim as soon as we could get there.

We found the restaurant easily enough—but it gave me the "willies" just to look at it. "He expects us to eat in there?" I asked in disbelief.

"Come on, Christine," Sally coaxed. "Where's your spirit of adventure?"

"I don't want to go in there," I said. "What if he's not there? We could get mugged."

The flashing neon lights in the window cast an eerie glow into the night. It looked like the kind of place a nice girl didn't want to be at that time of the morning. "Come on," Sally insisted.

I hesitantly followed her into a narrow, smoky, semi-dark storefront with maybe five booths, one, indeed, occupied by a bag lady. But there in the back was Tim Burke, waving us in. I thought, *At least we're safe. If we're with him, no one will bother us.*

"Nice restaurant, Tim," Sally said sarcastically as we took our seats. "Just the kind of place to bring a couple of girls you're trying to impress."

We all laughed, Tim more nervously than us.

When the waitress handed us the food-stained menus, I wished I'd worn gloves. But after we ordered breakfast and began to talk, I forgot all about my surroundings. Tim was full of questions about where I lived, where I had gone to school, what I did. When I told him about my current part-time job teaching dance routines to cheerleaders at a school for the deaf, he had a lot of questions about that.

Sally had her own agenda. She plied Tim with questions as if she was trying to decide whether he was worthy of me. She was so obvious that I felt a little embarrassed. I thought, *I'm a big girl. I can ask my own questions.*

When the jukebox kicked on, Tim turned and grinned. "The Beach Boys," he said.

"I like them, too," I said. And the conversation moved easily to music and entertainment. We found we had similar tastes.

When I mentioned I liked Barbra Streisand, Tim said he really liked her, too. "You remind me of her," he added.

"What do you mean?"

"Well, . . . uh, your nose."

I inhaled sharply. *Oh, no!* I thought.*That was my nickname in junior high school. 'Nose.'*

Tim obviously noted my surprise and embarrassment. "I'm sorry," he said. "I meant that as a compliment. I think noses are interesting. And I like yours a lot."

"You're kidding."

"No. I mean it."

Is this guy nuts or what? This is too good to be true, I thought. *I've heard of "leg men," but never "nose men."* Yet Tim seemed sincere. A really nice guy. I was enjoying talking with him. I had had my doubts at first, but . . . *So far, so good.*

Until the waitress brought us the check.

Tim

I SUDDENLY FELT SICK WITH EMBARRASSMENT. I HADN'T EVEN thought about it when I'd asked Christine and her friend to breakfast, but I had no cash left.

I had come to Lincoln with a $150 check made out to me, planning to cash it earlier at a local bank. But I had forgotten, and now I was out of money—with no possibility of cashing my check at 3 A.M. on Sunday morning, and no way of paying for breakfast. So much for impressing Christine.

As humiliating as it was, I had no choice but to offer an apology and admit my predicament. I even pulled out the uncashed check to support my story. When the girls looked at each other, I imagined what they were thinking: *First he brings us to a dive like this in the middle of the night. Then he sticks us with the check.*

But they were very nice about it. "No problem; don't worry about it," Sally said, insisting on paying for the whole thing. Then she invited me to follow them back to her friend's apartment. "It's almost dawn anyway," she said. "We may as well play cards or backgammon until morning."

Christine
♥♥♥♥♥

WHILE TIM WAS SO GENTLEMANLY AND EVERYTHING SEEMED ON the up and up, I might have thought twice when he couldn't pay in the restaurant. But he acted so genuinely embarrassed that I felt bad for him. In a funny sort of way, I think the breakfast-check incident added a little to his charm. And while I would never have invited him back to the apartment with us, I can't say I felt terribly sorry that Sally was forward enough to try to keep our encounter alive. The three of us had a great time playing backgammon and talking until 7:30 or 8:00 in the morning.

At that point, I remember going into the back room and motioning for Sally. "I really need to be heading back to Omaha," I whispered. "I told my mom I'd be home this morning."

"Let's make sure he leaves with you," she said. "Maybe the two of you can go out to eat."

"We just ate!" I reminded her. Besides, I figured Tim would be too embarrassed to mooch another meal.

"Well, you can just go somewhere together then."

"How am I going to work that?" I asked her.

"Just announce that you have to leave now. And I'll say something like, 'It was nice you could come, Tim.' That way he'll leave with you, and you'll just naturally end up together."

So when we went back into the living room, I said, "I'm really beat. I think I need to be heading home."

Sally jumped in right on cue. "Well, it was really great you guys could come. It was good to meet you, Tim." She practically pushed us toward the door together.

"I need to get back, too," Tim told me. "And I hate for you to have to go by yourself. Is it okay if you kind of follow me?"

"Okay, sure," I said. I winked at Sally, and she said good-bye. "But I need to gas up before I head home," I added.

"So do I," he responded. "Why don't you follow me?"

I pulled up to the gas pump at the first station we came to, and Tim immediately jumped out to fill my tank. "I'll get it," he insisted.

I thought, *What a gentleman!*

"One more thing," Tim said as he topped off my tank. He got a big, embarrassed grin on his face. "You're not going to believe this one . . ."

He had the same sheepish look I'd seen in the restaurant. So I asked, "What is it? You don't have money for gas?"

"If I had just five dollars' worth, I think I'd be fine. I promise to pay you back."

I began to laugh. "I think I can handle five dollars," I answered.

He finished pumping his gas, and I handed him the money to pay. As he walked toward the station, I called out, "Hey, Tim. Anything else I can buy for you?" He laughed.

When he came back out, he asked where he could call me to make arrangements to pay me back. I fought back a grin as I thought, *Pretty sly way to ask for a girl's phone number.*

I followed him as he drove onto the interstate. All the way to Omaha, I could see Tim constantly staring back at me in his rearview mirror. *Gee*, I thought, *I'd better be careful. I don't want to do anything embarrassing.*

For the next hour, I stayed on the bumper of Tim's '72 Monte Carlo, watching the back of his head and reliving the last few eventful hours. His awkward shyness. His embarrassment over the money. *He even likes my nose. He wasn't just saying that.*

I quickly decided I could be very interested in Tim Burke. But as we approached Omaha and the interstate split, he turned one way and I went the other—wondering if I would ever see him again.

As I walked in the front door of our home, Mom was working in the kitchen. "You're home early," she observed.

"You're not going to believe this," I told her. "I've got to tell you about my night. Just give me a minute." I went back to my room and changed into my pajamas and robe. As I carried my pillow into the kitchen, Mom asked how my trip had gone. I was so exhausted, I stretched out on the kitchen floor before I answered her. "I met a really, really nice guy there, Mom. His name is Tim, and he's from Omaha. I think you would like him. I've never met anyone quite like him. He's just the kindest, most gentlemanly guy. He seems so much older than he is."

"Just how old is he?"

"Don't worry, Mom," I answered with a laugh. "He's only 21." *Just 2 years older than me,* I thought. "But he seems so mature."

I started to tell her about meeting him and going out for breakfast. "He was just so polite."

"Do you think he'll call?" Mom asked.

"He promised he would. He owes me five dollars."

"What do you mean he owes you five dollars?"

"I loaned him gas money so he could get back home."

I explained about his check, laughing at the memory of his embarrassment.

"You think he's a real gentleman, but he didn't have money to pay for breakfast or gas?" Mom said.

"He really is, Mom. Trust me. I'll tell you more about him later. I'm just too tired right now." I still remember the skeptical look on my mother's face. It was the last thing I saw before falling asleep on the kitchen floor.

Tim

I FELT EMBARRASSED ASKING CHRISTINE IF I COULD BORROW GAS money. But it was nothing like my initial humiliation in the restaurant. After all, she already knew I was broke. And on the positive side, I figured that owing her five bucks would give me a legitimate reason to see her again right away.

I spent most of the drive back to Omaha watching her in my rearview mirror and thinking I'd never met a girl quite like her. Not only was she good-looking, but her warm, upbeat, and bubbly personality was also appealing and intriguing. She was so open, confident, and outgoing—so different from me. She was so much like what I wished I could be.

When we went our separate ways back in Omaha, I had to fight the urge to rush to the phone and call her. I took a nap instead. But after I woke up, I called to ask Christine if I could come by that evening to repay her loan and maybe take her out to dinner.

She said yes without even asking if I had the money to cover it. So we went out and talked for six or seven hours straight. We talked about things I had never told anyone before.

By the time the evening was over, I realized I had never felt about anyone the way I felt about Christine. I was crazy about her.

Christine

TIM WAS UNLIKE ANY GUY I HAD EVER DATED. HE ASKED ME SO many questions, as if he was really interested in me as a person. He wanted to know all about me and my childhood.

I told him that probably the strangest thing about my growing up was all the time I spent in the hospital. "It took years for the doctors to put me back together after a car accident broke my neck," I said.

"You're kidding," he said. "How old were you?"

"Fourteen."

"What happened?"

I told the story, including the fact that the driver of our car had been killed.

"Where did it happen? What year?"

When I told him, Tim said, "I knew the driver. He went to school with me." Then he deluged me with questions about my recovery. I told him how hard it was, how I'd learned to fight when I really felt like quitting. He seemed genuinely interested, and I enjoyed his attentiveness.

Finally I asked if he had ever been through anything hard like that. He got a real serious look on his face and nodded. "When my mom died," he said. We spent several minutes talking about the most painful episode of his life.

By the time we finally got back to my home that Sunday night, Mom had gone to bed. So I invited Tim in, and we talked some more. He was so easy to talk to. After he told me a little about his mother's death, I thought, *Here's a guy who knows what it's like to feel pain.*

The way he listened so intently and the way he looked at me, it was as if his eyes were saying, "You're really special." It gave me a sense of acceptance and affirmation that washed over and through me—clear down to my thirsty soul. It touched my heart, and I thought, *I don't know what I'm doing to impress him so much, but I've gotta keep it up. I just hope he never finds out what I'm really like.* I was convinced, *Here is a guy who could really understand and care for me.*

As it got terribly late, we both admitted the night before was catching up to us. It was time for Tim to leave. I walked him to the door, sensing his sudden uncertainty and awkwardness. He turned at the front step and said, "I really had a terrific time tonight. Would it be okay if I called you tomorrow?" I was impressed again by his politeness.

"Well, sure," I said.

He paused and looked even more awkward. "Uh, would it be all right if I gave you a good-night kiss?"

"Sure," I replied, tilting my face upward as he leaned down and gave me a sweet little peck on the cheek.

Wow! Part of me felt incredibly flattered to be treated with such gentle chivalry. But at the same time, a painful thought seared my soul: *I'm not the innocent princess he's acting as if I am. He doesn't really know the kind of person I've been, or he would just grab me and kiss me without giving it a thought.*

It was Tim's off-season, and I was still between jobs, so we had plenty of time for each other. We spent almost every day together during the next week—maybe as much as 60 or 70 hours in all. The more I was with Tim, the more I got to know him and the better I liked him.

It wasn't just a physical attraction (though I thought he was certainly good-looking). I had never known a guy who seemed to care about me and about knowing me as much as Tim did. From that first night, when we talked so honestly about the hardest things we had ever faced in our lives, he seemed so easy to share with.

We probably spent as much time together that first week as many couples do during months of dating. Most of our time was spent talking about anything and everything. So it seemed pretty natural the following weekend when Tim began saying things like, "I think I would like to spend the rest of my life with you."

While I certainly wasn't ready to set a wedding date or even think about rings, I wasn't put off by Tim's seeming eagerness for commitment. My biggest uncertainties, my only real doubts, were about me, not him. I still couldn't believe someone as wonderful and sweet as Tim could think I was so special and see so much good in me.

If I saw anything negative about Tim at all, anything that should have made me cautious, it was his drinking. The first couple of weekends we were together, he and his sister threw big parties, and I remember thinking, *What a fun family!* But as the weeks went by, I realized, *They do this every weekend!* I hadn't grown up around alcohol and had never been much of a drinker. I wasn't sure how I would adjust to that part of Tim's life.

Everywhere we went, everything we did, Tim always had something to drink. Even when we went to the zoo one afternoon, he poured Southern Comfort into his soft drink. Yet during those first few months, I didn't think Tim's drinking was a serious problem. Although he often got high, he never got loud or obnoxious, no matter how much he drank. I would know when he was high, but he would never get "sloppy drunk." Sometimes it made him a little more talkative, but he seemed to stay pretty much under control.

While I never tried to keep up with Tim's drinking, I did find myself drinking more than I ever had before. And I discovered what seemed like a very positive side effect: The more I drank, the more it masked the neck and back pain I lived with every day.

That made the arrival of the 1981 baseball season even more jarring. Tim had become an irreplaceable part of my life, the central focus of my everyday existence. Then one day in February, I had to pack him off to Florida for spring training, knowing he wouldn't be back for seven long months.

CHAPTER FOUR

Big Trouble

Christine
♥♥♥♥♥

I CAME HOME FROM TAKING TIM TO THE AIRPORT FEELING AS IF someone had just died. Suddenly there was a huge emptiness in my life—a dark, gaping hole big enough to swallow me and half of Nebraska. I remember unlocking the door, walking inside, and grabbing my little cockapoo, Benji. He tried to console me as I thought, *I don't know how I'm going to do this.* When Tim was assigned for the 1981 season to the Pirates' A team (the lowest level of professional baseball) in Alexandria, Virginia, he may as well have been a million miles from Omaha.

Of course, we frequently talked on the phone. But it wasn't the same. And soon I felt a growing distance between us that I didn't think could be blamed on the miles or the phone lines separating us. Tim seldom seemed his usual warm and loving self.

"What's wrong?" I asked.

"Nothing. I'm okay," he assured me. There was a closed sense of tightness, a tension I had never felt before. And when I pressed him for an explanation, Tim was unwilling or unable to talk. He was strangely quiet and different.

For a while, I told myself it was probably just the pressure of his first full season of professional baseball, exaggerated by our sudden lack of time together and the frustration of maintaining our relationship over the telephone. So I took time off from the bridal shop where I worked and made two trips to Alexandria, Virginia, that summer. Tim paid my way.

The first trip was particularly memorable. I had looked forward to seeing Tim play for the first time, so I had fun finally watching him pitch. I remember going to the ballpark (if you could call it a "park") and thinking, *This is professional baseball?*

You've got to be kidding. It was a rinky-dink field next to a school. The place didn't even have locker rooms; players changed in a school classroom where the desks had been pushed against the wall. The conditions of A ball shocked me.

Tim didn't start the last game I attended on that trip. I sat with other girlfriends and wives in the second row on the third-base side of the field. We were chatting away when a batter for the Winston-Salem Red Sox broke his bat on a swing that sent the bat's barrel sailing toward the third-base stands. As the fans around us ducked, I looked up just in time to see a big, solid chunk of hardwood tumbling end over end. I instinctively turned to cover my face—but I wasn't fast enough to keep the bat from hitting me squarely in the head.

The next thing I knew, I was lying face up on the ground with a circle of faces hovering over me. Tim had seen the whole thing from the dugout. He had run across the diamond, jumped over the fence into the stands, and taken my hand. Now he was asking, "Are you awake? Are you okay?"

"Yeah," I moaned. "What happened?" A surging river of pain running from my head down through my neck made it impossible to move.

Someone yelled, "Get the ambulance!" Soon a gate opened in the center-field fence, and an ambulance drove across the grass and through the infield, stopping next to the third-base dugout. When Tim told the paramedics I had a cervical fusion, they knew that the wrong kind of blow to the head or neck could cause permanent paralysis. So they immobilized my neck and gingerly strapped me onto a stretcher.

The game was halted for more than 15 minutes as I was carefully loaded into the ambulance and driven slowly back across the field. Even though my neck hurt so much I could hardly see straight, I kept telling Tim, "I'm okay. I'll be all right."

As we eased out through the center-field gate, I even joked, "They'll never forget me here. Let's see you ever try to bring another girl to this ballpark." Tim laughed.

I only sustained a slight concussion from the incident, but I went home from that introduction to minor-league baseball wearing a neck brace and suffering from excruciating pain.

I planned both my visits to Alexandria with great anticipation and high hopes of regaining whatever our relationship had lost. But each time I went to Virginia, it quickly became apparent that Tim wasn't feeling the same frustration I was and didn't understand my concerns at all. While he was obviously glad to see me and made me feel as loved as ever, and even though we were together in person again, I still sensed a difference in him. He drank more than before. But now, instead of loosening him up and making him a little more talkative, the alcohol couldn't seem to ease the air of tightness and intensity I had never witnessed during the off-season.

I was as desperately in love with Tim as ever, but I went back home after each of my visits deeply disappointed. *Could this just be what baseball does to him?* I wondered. The thought really began to trouble me.

Tim

A LOT OF THINGS WERE GOING ON INSIDE ME THAT SUMMER. BUT since I didn't really understand them myself, I couldn't articulate them to Christine or even begin to see their implications in our relationship.

Alexandria was my first real experience with professional baseball. Despite the grueling bus rides, the cheap motels, the fast-food diet, and night after night of playing baseball in ancient, dirty, poorly lit, small-town ballparks, there was an almost indescribable sense of excitement about the experience.

Minor-league baseball demanded an all-consuming focus never required of me before. At the same time, there was a sense of freedom in having nothing else in the world to do except play the sport I loved. From the time I first stepped on the mound in Little League through my college career, I might have said, "Baseball is my life." But there were always other responsibilities and requirements placed on me—at school, at home, and just growing up.

Now, suddenly, as a full-time professional baseball player,

there was nothing else. No classes to attend. No homework to do. No chores at home. No family to answer to. Nothing to do but play baseball and get paid for doing it—a million kids' dream come true.

Sharing the dream with me was a team of other guys in the same situation. So the rigors of the minor-league back roads became an adventure joined by like-minded comrades who also reveled in the opportunity to eat, sleep, talk, and think baseball 24 hours a day—and plenty of free time to fill up with drinking.

I certainly didn't love Christine any less. I missed her desperately all season. The highlights of my summer were her visits to Virginia. But looking back, I can see how my narrowing focus on baseball naturally affected our relationship and our already-poor communication patterns.

However, one thing I learned quickly that summer was the importance of focusing totally on baseball, and the possible consequences if I didn't. As exciting and fun as it seemed, minor-league baseball was definitely more than a game; it was also a business. Players came and went in revolving-door fashion. Those who performed stayed. Those who didn't were quickly cut and gone. And most players cut at the A level had nowhere to go but home, their professional baseball careers over.

On a personal level, I didn't have any immediate fear of getting cut. I had been a high draft choice, and it was my first season. The Pirates had enough invested in me to show a little patience. But as I watched player after player clean out his locker and walk away knowing he had reached the end of his lifelong dream to play professional baseball, I began to sense a pressure I had never known before. I knew the time would soon come when I had to perform on the field or my own dreams would be shattered. I tried to imagine what life would be like without baseball, but I couldn't. The thought was too horrible to dwell on.

I suppose that's part of the reason I stayed drunk so much that summer. It relieved the pressure.

More than that, though, drinking had long provided a bond between me and my friends, and now it served the same purpose among my new teammates. The fact that I was on my own for the first time, combined with my role as a starting pitcher (which required that I play only once every four or five days), led me to fall into what became a predictable pattern. On nights I pitched, I would go out after the game and get really drunk as celebration or consolation, depending on how I had thrown that night. I would keep drinking pretty heavily over the next two or three days before easing up in time to feel ready for my next pitching assignment. Then I would begin the cycle all over again.

I shared an apartment with three other players that summer. We met at spring training, and when we all were assigned to Alexandria, we decided to save money by living together. With all the time we spent living, traveling, and playing together, we quickly became friends as well as drinking buddies.

Sometime that July, I got my first truly bitter taste of the business side of baseball. That's when one of my roommates, Joe Fiori, the best defensive second baseman who had ever played behind me, was released. One day he was there with us, probably my closest friend on the team; the next day, he packed his bags and left town. Just like that, a friend was gone, and I didn't know if I would ever see him again.

I lost another drinking buddy that season under circumstances that upset me even more at the time. When Joe left, my roommates and I took in another player to help with the rent. The new guy, Kerry Keenan, was an outspoken Christian who seemed eager to talk about his faith. I let him know up front that I wasn't interested in any of his God talk, but he found a ready listener in our roommate, Rich Leggatt. Before I knew it, Rich told me he'd been "born again" and began turning down my invitations to go out on the town. Instead of the nightly escapades we had enjoyed on the local bar scene earlier in the summer, Rich stayed home. I would wake up mornings to find Rich already up and reading a Bible. I couldn't believe it. I often got angry and yelled at him, telling him how stupid I thought he was. "We used to have so much fun together," I said. "Now look at you. You're so boring!"

Rich never snapped back. He wouldn't argue at all. That made me even madder.

It wasn't as though drinking was a problem, at least not for me—or so I thought. Professionally, I had a fairly good season pitching on a poor ball club. My won-lost record was only 8-10, but my other statistics were very respectable. I got positive feedback from the coaches and figured I had done well enough to be moved up to the AA level the following year. My career was progressing.

I couldn't see that my drinking was a problem personally, either. I realized things weren't quite the same between me and Christine. But that seemed natural enough since we were separated for so many months. My feelings for her certainly hadn't changed; I still wanted to marry her. And toward the end of the season, I could hardly wait to get back to her in Omaha.

Christine

WHEN TIM CAME HOME, I WAS THRILLED TO SEE HIM. WE WOULD have the entire off-season together, plenty of time to restore whatever our relationship had lost over the summer. After all, we loved each other more than ever.

Tim's drinking was an obvious problem to me. He spent more and more time under the influence, and his behavior began to bother me. I got extremely upset one night when we went to a county fair with friends. Tim got so drunk that he was hanging all over me on one of the rides. When I told him afterward how embarrassed I had been, he apologized. We talked about his drinking, and he promised to keep it under control.

But soon I found myself counting his beers whenever we were out. I didn't want to, but I couldn't help it. I knew he'd begin to get drunk after eight or nine beers, so the closer he got to that limit, the more upset I became. At one party, I got so angry that one of Tim's friend's asked me what was wrong. When I told him, his response was disturbingly casual. "Hey, Christine," he said, "you have to realize Tim's on his way to being a big baseball star. There's naturally going to be a lot of partying and socializing. When you're a pro athlete, that's just the way it is."

I remember thinking, *Well, it's not going to be that way with me. I'm not going to live like that.*

The issue came to a head one night that fall in Tim's basement apartment at his sister's rented house. (His father had remarried and moved to Southern California.) All evening I tried to slow Tim's drinking, but he got so drunk that he was on the verge of unconsciousness. There was no talking to him at that point. It was horrible. I stayed with him most of the night, sitting on the couch, watching him sleep and waiting for him to sober up.

I remember thinking, *I love Tim. He's the nicest guy I ever met. But I don't know how to deal with this.*

When he finally came around in the wee hours of the morning, I told him, "We need to talk. I love you so much, Tim. But I can't live like this with you drunk all the time. This has got to change— and if it doesn't, maybe it would be best for us to break up."

At some point, Tim exploded and screamed at me, "Don't you love me enough to help me?"

I tried to talk, but he became defensive, and we argued until I was so upset I stomped out. I stopped just outside the door and sank down on the steps. I loved Tim too much to just walk away.

A few moments later, Tim stormed out the door and past me, staggering down the street into the darkness until he disappeared. When he didn't return, I went looking for him and found him sitting on a curb a couple of blocks away. Without saying a word, I sat down beside him and put my arm around his shoulder.

I could see he was fighting back tears as he softly asked me, "Do you think I have a drinking problem?"

Instead of answering him, I turned the question around: "Do you think you have a drinking problem, Tim?"

He was quiet for a while. "Yeah, I think I do," he finally said. Then he added, "But I also think I love you enough to quit."

"You can't do it for me," I told him, "and I wouldn't want you to try. You have to decide to do it for yourself or you'll end up resenting me."

He couldn't imagine resenting me. He said he loved me too much. I assured him I didn't doubt his love and told him I loved him, too.

"Then will you help me?" He sounded so needy, so helpless, and so sincere.

"Yes," I told him, though I didn't know how I could. He wrapped his arms around me, and we sat for a time on that curb in the darkness just holding each other.

Tim did try to change. He would go several days without drinking anything alcoholic, but then suddenly his resolve would be gone and he would get drunk again. It seemed as if the longer he held out, the more determined he seemed, the more drunk he got when he finally gave in.

I don't know how many times during the off-season Tim apologized and promised to stop. I always let it go because I knew he was sincere. I had no doubt at all that he was truly trying to change. He obviously needed help. And while I had no idea how to give it, I couldn't bring myself to walk away and leave him.

Instead, I found reassurance in Tim's ongoing attempts to change. I convinced myself that the combination of his determination to change and our unquestionable love for each other would soon prevail. So in January 1982, when he asked me to marry him, I said, *"Yes!"* We set the date for October, after baseball season.

The excitement of our official engagement helped overpower any lingering doubts. Whenever I thought about Tim's drinking, I easily convinced myself, *It's going to be okay. It will change. Once we're married and together all the time, things will be better. When the baseball season doesn't separate us anymore, we'll be able to work on the problem together.*

By the time Tim left in February for spring training, I dreaded the thought of another summer separated from him. Though we talked every day on the phone, and Tim seemed more communicative than he had the previous season, I missed him desperately.

So I was ready when he called late one night the first month and told me how lonely he felt. "I can't take it anymore, Christine," he said. "I don't want to wait until October. Let's get married right away!"

I hung up the phone that night, turned to my mother, and asked, "Mom, how do you feel about small weddings?"

"Oh, brother!" she responded.

I immediately called my bridesmaids and told them, "Sorry, girls, but the October plans have been canceled. We're going to have a simple ceremony right away in whatever city Tim's assigned to this year."

At the end of spring training, the Pirates sent Tim to pitch for their AA team in Buffalo, so I began making plans to join him and get married there on May 5, 1982.

To say we had a simple wedding is a drastic understatement. We found a church that agreed to open its doors long enough for a wedding ceremony. Since Tim wasn't scheduled to pitch that night, his manager gave him the day off. Because the church wasn't unlocked, an hour before my wedding, I was standing in our apartment in a Buffalo suburb while my mother helped me into my wedding dress. She shook her head and said, "I never dreamed I'd ever be standing in an apartment in Cheektowaga, New York, dressing my daughter for her wedding."

A few minutes later, I rushed out to the car carrying my flowers and veil as a sunbather sprawled on the apartment lawn sat up and called, "What are you doing?"

"What do you think?" I shouted back. "I'm going to get married!" I scrunched myself and my big, fluffy wedding dress into mom's compact car and wished the entire world could share the joy I felt at that moment.

My mom was my matron of honor, and Tim's dad served as best man. The minister, whom we never saw again, performed a brief ceremony before a "crowd" made up of Tim's uncle, several of his teammates, and two players' wives. I remember laughing and saying at some point, "Somebody snap a picture or something." The only documentation we got was a couple of snapshots and a fuzzy movie shot with an old super-8 camera Tim's sister loaned him.

Before I knew it, we were pronounced husband and wife. We kissed and then hurried out of the church into a hail of rice. It's probably never a good idea to give a bunch of professional baseball players anything to throw at you. Those guys could wing the rice! As we made our escape, I told Tim, "I'll be picking grains of rice out of my skin for weeks."

The reception consisted of dinner with my mom, Tim's dad, and Tim's uncle in a nearby restaurant. Our honeymoon was a single night's stay in a local hotel. The next day, Tim left on a ten-day road trip with his team.

I was left to get settled in our apartment, contemplate my new, lifelong commitment, and adjust to the reality of married life. I was all alone in a city I'd never been to before, where I didn't know a single soul, with no job, and with nothing to do all day but stare at the bare walls of a nearly empty apartment, waiting for my daily long-distance phone call from the man who married me one day and left town the next.

By the second or third day, I called home and asked my mother, "What have I done? Whatever possessed me?"

I thought I would go crazy with loneliness before Tim got home from that road trip. I certainly had plenty of time to string "Welcome Home" banners and plan a big, special dinner for the night of his return. I couldn't wait to see him, hold him, talk to him.

When I heard his knock, I rushed to the door and flung it open. There stood Tim with a teammate who'd given him a ride home, looking a little embarrassed by the crepe-paper streamers I'd taped across the door for him to burst through. He said an awkward, self-conscious good-bye to his friend as he loosened one of the streamers and carefully high-stepped over another. He didn't even give me a real hug and kiss until his teammate had left and the door was closed.

Once he got lovey-dovey, I forgave his initial coolness. But his quietness during supper bothered me again. I wanted to talk, but Tim didn't. After dinner he got drunk, which made him even more quiet and withdrawn. He plopped down in front of the TV with the remote control and went from one channel to another.

"Can you turn that off, Honey?" I asked. "I really want to talk to you."

When he didn't respond, I got up and shut off the TV myself. "Do you still love me?" I asked. "Or did something happen these past two weeks? It's like you've become a different person who doesn't even care about me." I told him how discouraged and lonely I had been while he was gone, and how hurtful and frustrating it was to plan a special welcome-home celebration and have him spend the entire night drunk and untalkative.

I went to bed so angry and hurt that when he finally joined me, I told him that if things didn't change—and change fast—I might be better off going back to Omaha.

Tim had absorbed a number of my explosions during the course of our relationship, and whenever I had raised the possibility of breaking up, he had always begged me to stay. This time, however, he listened and then quietly replied, "Maybe you should go back home."

His words felt like arrows piercing my heart. There seemed to be nothing left to say.

We had had problems before, but nothing like this. So it was hard to believe that after just two weeks of marriage, I was seriously considering walking out. And my husband saw so little hope that he thought maybe I should.

I lay in bed that night, the longest night of my life, thinking, *What's wrong with Tim? Or is it me? Maybe he's quit loving me because he finally figured out what I'm really like.*

I'd rather be dead.

CHAPTER FIVE

The Search

Tim

MARRIAGE SEEMED TO HAVE CHANGED EVERYTHING. DID I KNOW what I was getting into? I certainly didn't know what Christine expected of me.

I had wanted to get married because I loved her. We had shared so much and grown so close in such a short time that I knew I wanted to spend the rest of my life with Christine. But I can't say I had a very clear understanding of the implications of marriage.

We had our share of problems during the year and a half we were dating. But our love remained strong, and we became each other's best friend. So I figured everything would settle down and be easier once we actually got married.

My own expectations were fairly simple. I wanted to play ball, drink with my friends, and have fun with Christine. Dating her seemed so easy and comfortable. So while I had heard people say marriage is a lot of work, I guess I expected our life together to be one long party.

Christine had different ideas—and she hit me with a pile of them when I got home from that first road trip. She accused me of not wanting to talk to her anymore, and of not listening. She said, "I'm all alone here in Buffalo. I have no friends here, no family, no job. I need someone to talk to. I need you to care about me and to communicate with me. But you've changed. You're not even gentle and loving anymore. When you have a bad game, you're harsh and cold, and you won't talk. I can't survive like this. I need to know what's going on inside you, how you feel. I feel like I'm all by myself here, and if you keep drinking, it's going to destroy us. That's not the way to deal with any problem."

In other words, what I heard her saying was, "This marriage isn't what I expected. Maybe it was all a big mistake."

I still loved Christine very much. But I thought, *Maybe she's right. Maybe it was a big mistake. This marriage seems to have so many demands, so many responsibilities. Christine evidently needs more than I have to give her.*

So when she threatened to leave me and go back to Omaha, I didn't know what else to say except, "Maybe you should." But it tore me up to say it.

I went to the ballpark that day feeling hurt and confused. I guess it showed because a couple of my teammates asked, "What's wrong, Tim?"

I didn't want to talk about it, but I didn't want to lie, either. So I admitted, "Christine's packing to go back home to Omaha. Our marriage just isn't working out."

When Kerry Keenan heard that (he had been promoted from Alexandria to Buffalo along with me), he pulled me aside. "Tim," he said, "if you and Christine can just hang in there another 24 hours, there's a Bible study tomorrow for players and their wives. If you would be willing to talk to the pastor and his wife who lead our Bible study, I think they might be able to help you."

I told him I would think about it. I didn't want to go to a Bible study. But then, what did I have to lose? While I was reluctantly willing to try anything at that point, I didn't know how Christine would react to the idea. In fact, I wasn't sure she would still be there when I got back to the apartment.

Christine
♥♥♥♥♥

WHEN TIM CAME HOME AND TOLD ME ABOUT THE INVITATION TO a Bible study, I can't say I was very excited. I could still recall the bitterness I felt after the accident—a deep-rooted, malignant anger that had eaten into and hardened my heart.

If God didn't care enough back then to protect me from all that pain, what did He care about my marriage? Reluctantly, however, I decided that going to a Bible study, even talking to a pastor, couldn't make things any worse than we had messed them up already. And because I desperately loved Tim and didn't really want to leave him, it would give me an excuse to quit packing and stay another day. I told Tim, "Okay, I'll give it a chance." I was that desperate.

That next day, we walked across the complex to the player's apartment where the Bible study group met. I remember nervously thinking, *What if I have to find a specific verse and don't know where to look? What if they expect us to pray? I won't know what to say.*

Only four or five couples attended, along with the pastor and his wife—Bill and Charlotte—who led the study. I don't remember what passage they read that day or exactly what was said during the study itself. But I do remember wondering if they had all conspired to aim the entire study directly at me. Everything they read out of the Bible seemed to hit me right between the eyes.

It amazed me that here I had thought I *was* a Christian, yet I discovered that being raised by a Christian mother didn't make me one. Occasional church attendance didn't make me one, either. I began to understand what being a Christian is really all about.

I wanted to hear more, so when Bill and Charlotte asked Tim and me if they could talk with us alone after the study, I eagerly agreed. Afterward, they went back to our apartment with us for a visit.

Tim

LIKE CHRISTINE, I DON'T REMEMBER MANY DETAILS ABOUT THE Bible study itself, but I do remember our time afterward with Bill and Charlotte. As they opened their Bibles again in our apartment and began talking about what Jesus said and taught, I distinctly remember thinking, *Wow! This is all new to me!*

I had grown up going to Mass every week. I knew Jesus was the Son of God. I believed the Bible was true. I just never bothered to read it. I always figured I was a pretty nice guy. If God graded on the curve, I thought, *Gee, I must be better than half the people in the world. I'll make it to heaven.*

But Bill and Charlotte said that just knowing the facts and trying to live a better life than most people wasn't enough. Backing up every point with Scripture, they insisted God wanted faith to make a difference in every area of our lives.

"The Lord wants to help you build better, more positive relationships with others," they told us. "He can heal and strengthen your marriage. His Word can give you guidance that will help you make the rough decisions you face in life. Being a Christian can even have an impact on how you pursue your career—on the baseball field and off."

Bill and Charlotte went on to talk about having a "relationship" with Jesus where He becomes a friend and not some distant God. They explained what it meant to be "born again" (John 3:3), making clear what I'd never understood before. They turned to Scripture after Scripture—passages like Romans 3:23, which showed us that everyone has sinned. They pointed out that we needed to repent by asking God to forgive our sins and then turning away from the wrong things we had been doing (see Luke 13:3). And they added that it wasn't enough just to say "I'm sorry" and vow to change; we needed to be willing to give up control of our lives to God and let His teachings guide our decisions (see John 14:15).

According to the Scriptures Bill and Charlotte showed us, we couldn't really become Christians until we did that. While it all sounded new to me, a lot of what they said made sense. I certainly couldn't argue with the "we're all sinners" part. And I understood forgiveness. But I had a little more trouble with the idea of "knowing God personally." Christine and I both had questions about exactly what that meant. And the idea of "giving God control of your life" sounded pretty fanatical. When they talked about "letting the Lord be Lord of your life," it sounded even more strange and serious.

They admitted it was a very serious decision. They repeatedly emphasized the importance of thinking it through, because what God wants from people is a total commitment of their lives.

What they said certainly intrigued me. But the idea of giving up my life was a problem. I wasn't ready to do that.

Christine
♥♥♥♥♥

I KNEW I HAD NEVER REPENTED THE WAY BILL AND CHARLOTTE were talking about. I had never specifically said, "Lord, I'm sorry for all my sins." I didn't know I needed to—until Bill read me what Jesus said: "Repent, or you will perish." I was beginning to understand that I needed to tell God I was sorry and start living to please Him. Yet I wondered what would happen once I did that. I asked Bill, "Will I turn into some fanatical fruitcake?"

He laughed and answered, "No, you'll still be Christine—just with Jesus inside, helping you live the kind of life He wants for you."

Bill and Charlotte went on to ask us to let them know when we were willing to commit our lives to God, and they would be happy to pray with us and help us. We could even do it that night if we were ready.

It all sounded so nice. But we weren't ready.

"We'll think about it," we promised as our visitors left for home.

I didn't go back to Omaha that week. Or the next. Or the next. I didn't make a conscious decision to stay; I just didn't follow through on my plans to leave. It certainly wasn't because our marriage improved; it didn't. It wasn't because Tim changed, either; he didn't. It also wasn't because I found great reason to hope in what Bill and Charlotte told us about how God wanted to help us if we were willing to commit our lives to Him. That still seemed so drastic.

Another friend who was a Christian helped me get a better understanding of commitment, however, with this analogy: "Okay, Christine, let's think about your marriage for a minute. How do you think Tim would feel if you said to him, 'For 361 days a year, I'll be a faithful wife to you. But you'll just have to understand that on those other four days, there will be Bill, Tom, Joe, and Ted'? How many husbands are going to be satisfied with a relationship like that? That's not true, total commitment. Total commitment is what God wants from us, too."

Tim and I met with Bill and Charlotte several times during the next few weeks. We spent a lot of time reading the Bible and try-ing to understand the passages they explained to us. I looked for-ward to the times Tim and I would read the Bible together and discuss its meaning as we understood it. Those seemed to be the only times we really communicated with each other.

We usually came up with a stream of questions we wanted answered the next time we met with our spiritual counselors. They were patient with us but very consistent and clear. This was no easy, flippant decision they asked us to consider. They weren't promising us some sort of spiritual aspirin to solve the problems in our lives. We had to be serious. God was there—loving us, ready and waiting to be a part of our lives. But it was our deci-sion. We had to be willing to repent, to turn from our sins, and to commit our entire lives to Him.

We still weren't ready.

One night, Bill and Charlotte pulled out a piece of paper and asked us to list all the sins we could remember committing. I thought, *You don't have enough paper.* Then they made another list on the right side of the paper, including things like peace, joy, love, patience, contentment, and a few other things they said were all benefits of knowing and following God. "Maybe you think this second list looks a little boring compared to the first," they said. "But the further you go in life, the longer you live, the more you will realize these are the things that really matter. These are the things that will make you happy."

We certainly weren't happy the way we were. I had to admit that. But . . .

Tim

THE MORE I READ THE BIBLE THAT SUMMER, AND THE MORE I heard from Bill and Charlotte, the more I thought, *If what the Bible says is true, why haven't I heard this before? Maybe I heard it but wasn't listening.*

I can't say that all the time I spent reading and discussing the Bible that summer made an immediate difference in my life. I was searching but still struggling. Christine hadn't left me, but I knew she was still miserable. Our marriage was a mess, and so were we. I continued my old pattern of drinking and emotional withdrawal whenever I turned in a poor pitching performance. And there seemed to be a lot of them.

I was probably drinking at least as much as ever. The only difference now was that I felt as if God were looking over my shoulder and taking all the fun out of my sin. So I was living the way I had been but not enjoying it as much. That frustrated me.

But I didn't see how I could ever change. I decided I could never be good enough to be a Christian.

When I told that to Bill, he assured me, "You don't have to change *before* you become a Christian. If you're willing to commit your life to God, He will accept you and forgive you just the way you are. Then He'll give you the strength to make the necessary changes."

Still, I felt as though I'd be signing away my life. I had dreams and goals I didn't want to give up.

"God knows what's best for your life, Tim," Bill assured me. "That's what He wants you to have."

I certainly wasn't doing well on my own. It wasn't just personally and in my marriage, either. For the first time in my entire athletic career, I was floundering on the field. I had started the season strong, posting four wins and only one loss before beginning a downward spiral.

A number of future big leaguers were on our team in Buffalo that year, including Rafael Belliard, Mike Bielecki, and Steve Farr. But we had a horrible team with one of the worst records in minor-league baseball. I contributed to the poor team effort by finishing with an unacceptable 7-10 record and an embarrassing 5.19 ERA, more than two runs higher than the 3.00 ERA I would have considered passable.

For the first time in my baseball career, I began to worry that maybe I wasn't going to make it. Maybe I didn't have what it takes to be a major-league pitcher. With those doubts came a new degree of pressure: *If I don't perform, if I don't turn things around, I may be gone. If I can't cut it in AA, how long are the*

Pirates going to stick with me?

As the pressure continued to build, I happened across a Bible verse that practically jumped off the page at me. First Peter 5:7 said, "Cast all your anxiety on him because he cares for you."

Wow! If God really cares about my drinking problem, my messed-up marriage, and my lousy pitching, He must really love me.

That thought hit me hard. For a couple of days after I read it, I couldn't get it out of my mind.

On August 25, I woke up thinking about that verse, asking myself, *Why am I so reluctant to give God control of my life?* It wasn't as though I was doing such a great job. I had turned it into a terrible mess, while God had never made a mistake. What were the odds He was going to make His first mistake on me? He could easily do better with my life than I was doing.

I looked over at Christine lying next to me in bed. She was awake. "I can't run from God anymore," I told her. "I think I'm ready to do what Bill and Charlotte have been talking about. If I wait until I'm good enough, it will never happen. So He will just have to take me the way I am. I'm ready to give Jesus control of my life and become a Christian."

What I didn't know was that Christine had reached a similar point in her spiritual struggle. She awoke that morning and came to the same decision on her own.

"Me, too," she said.

CHAPTER SIX

Fears and Tears

Christine
♥♥♥♥♥

WHEN WE PHONED BILL AND CHARLOTTE LATER THAT MORNING to say we were ready to make a serious commitment, they invited us over to talk face to face. Even as we drove to meet them at their church, I felt an incredible sense of anticipation: *I'm going to get forgiven!*

They greeted us with friendly hugs. "You understand what we're talking about?" Bill asked.

Tim and I looked at each other and nodded. We summarized what we had learned in our summer-long process of study and searching. We knew we were sinners and needed to turn away from the wrong we had been doing. We believed God really did know what was best for us, so we needed to make our decisions and live our lives based on what the Bible teaches. Tim added that he understood baseball had been the number one priority in his life, and that had to change because God wanted first place in our hearts. He wanted us to give Him control of our entire lives.

"Are you ready to do that right now?" Bill asked. "Repent? Commit your lives to Christ wherever He takes you? Admit you can't live a Christian life without God's help and presence in your daily lives?"

"Yes," we replied.

So Bill prayed, telling God what we wanted to do. Then he asked us to tell God for ourselves. I don't remember everything I prayed, but the gist of it was, "Lord, please forgive me for all the bad things I've done. I want to live the way you want me to. Help me do that."

It all seemed so simple. I can't say I felt a big emotional rush at that point.

When we finished praying, we were baptized. As Tim and I donned white robes and stepped one at a time down into the baptistry, the symbolism seemed powerfully significant. I felt an almost tangible force when I heard the words, "Christine Burke, I baptize you in the name of the Father, the Son, and the Holy Spirit." The cool water closed over my face, and I held my breath. When I was lifted up again, my heart practically soared. As the water from my hair streamed over my face and shoulders, I felt cleaner and more free than I ever remembered. *Is this what it feels like to be forgiven?* I wondered. *I feel so pure and clean.*

Explaining our decision to us, Bill used a simple analogy: "When you become a Christian, you're a new person in God's eyes [see 2 Corinthians 5:17]. He forgives your past, wipes your old slate clean, and gives you a brand-new start."

I felt that fresh, amazing newness as I came up out of the water. I knew it was true. My life was going to be different.

As I tried to articulate my feelings to Tim during the drive home, words just didn't seem adequate. But we both knew that without a doubt we had made the right decision—the most important decision of our lives.

However, even before we reached our apartment, reality knocked me off my spiritual high. As Tim made a quick turn, the Pepsi I was drinking sloshed out on my shoes and all over the floor. I let fly with a slew of cuss words before I caught myself. *So much for the new, improved me*, I thought. I felt horribly guilty.

"Uh-oh," Tim teased, "your slate's not clean anymore!"

Then I began laughing. Fortunately, our friends had warned us that becoming Christians wouldn't make us perfect people who never sin. "But when you do," they said, "it's important for you to stop right then and ask forgiveness again."

So that's what I did. I prayed right there in the car, asking God to forgive my language and help me do a better job of controlling my mouth in the future. The terrible feeling of guilt was gone as quickly as it had arrived.

As embarrassed as I was to find myself swearing on the way home from becoming a Christian, I see now how that incident reinforced a valuable lesson for Tim and me by setting an important precedent in our new relationship with God. We are still going to make mistakes, but when we do—as soon as we do—we can go to God knowing He will gladly forgive us and wipe our slates clean again and again and again.

Tim

WE CERTAINLY DIDN'T BECOME PERFECT PEOPLE. BUT WE EXPERIENCED two significant and immediate changes.

One was Christine's attitude toward our marriage. Though we still had problems, she no longer thought of leaving. After I got home from that first road trip, she had been ready to walk out. The possibility of her leaving hung heavy on my mind throughout the summer because tensions remained so high. But when we became Christians, divorce no longer seemed like an option to Christine. We were suddenly playing by a new set of rules. It was as if in making a commitment to God, she also made a commitment to our marriage. That in itself gave her hope that our relationship would improve.

The other encouraging change had to do with my drinking. Incredibly, my desire for alcohol—the daily drive to get drunk—which had been a major focus of my life for years, simply vanished. From the day I became a Christian, the old, familiar craving for alcohol was gone.

I knew that wasn't my doing. Many times I had tried to quit, and I had always failed. It had to be God's power in my life. It was if He was saying, "If you mean business with Me, Tim, I'll show you I mean business with you."

If He could do that for me, I was serious about wanting to live for Him. I was experiencing God's amazing love. But I soon realized I had a lot to learn.

Christine

I WOULDN'T HAVE BEEN COCKY ENOUGH TO ADMIT IT AT THE TIME, but when we made our commitment to Christ, I thought I would skyrocket spiritually while Tim would grow a lot slower and maybe even wither a bit. I expected to be the spiritual leader in our marriage who would drag and prod Tim along.

To my surprise, almost the opposite happened. I couldn't believe how serious Tim was about his faith. When we moved back to Omaha for the off-season, he was even more concerned than I was about finding a good church. And when we began attending Trinity Interdenominational Church, Tim learned one spiritual lesson after another.

If the Bible said it, Tim believed it and absorbed it like a sponge. I was the analytical one with all the questions, quibbling over details. When Tim learned that God wanted Christians to tithe, he was ready to start writing checks. I was the one asking, "How much? Net or gross?"

On one hand, Tim's new spiritual sensitivity encouraged and inspired me. I wished I could be more like him and trust God as he did. But on the other hand, I was troubled and embarrassed by my ongoing fears. Tim would get up in the morning and leave for his off-season job, and I would watch him go, thinking after he disappeared from sight, *What if he's in an accident? What if the car blows up? The phone's going to ring, and I'm going to learn that the man I love more than anyone in the world is gone. My life will be changed forever. How will I live with that?*

I would tell myself, *You're a Christian now. You shouldn't be afraid like that.* But when I couldn't talk myself out of it, I went in to talk to our pastor in Omaha.

"I don't think your problem is fear, Christine," he said. "I think it's trust. You need to learn to trust God." He even read me Proverbs 3:5: "Trust in the LORD with all your heart and lean not on your own understanding."

But I remember thinking, *You're nuts.* If God allowed my accident, if He allowed my father to leave, if He allowed all the bad things that had happened in my life, how could I ever trust Him? I just couldn't be as trusting as Tim.

Yet during the '82-'83 off-season, I learned that Tim battled fears of his own.

Tim

THAT WINTER, WE WERE LIVING IN THE BASEMENT OF CHRISTINE'S mom's house when I got a call from the Pirates' minor-league director. "We just traded you [along with three other minor leaguers] to the New York Yankees for Lee Mazilli," he said.

Oh, man! I thought. I had spent my entire life rooting *against* the Yankees. My only real friends in baseball—and they were good friends—were in the Pirates' organization. So in spite of the chance at a fresh start, I felt terrible about the trade.

I knew the pressure I felt the previous summer in Buffalo was nothing compared to what I would face walking into spring training with a new organization. At least the Pirates had invested a second-round draft pick and a nice signing bonus in me. To the Yankees, however, I was almost an afterthought—just one of four unknown minor leaguers they had taken in a trade for a part-time veteran in the twilight of his career. I knew that if I didn't pitch well, 1983 could be my last season in professional baseball.

Christine
♥♥♥♥♥

SOMETHING OBVIOUSLY WAS TROUBLING TIM. ANY TIME WE TALKED about the big leagues, I could see a quiet intensity on his face, almost an obsession in his eyes. So one dark winter evening, sitting in my mother's basement (the only place we could afford to live that off-season), I asked Tim what was wrong. He tried to shrug it off as nothing more than a bad mood, but I kept pressing. Finally he admitted he was worried about spring training and the upcoming season.

"Is making it to the major leagues what's bothering you? Is that it?" I asked. "You seem so tense and tight. So stressed."

"If I don't do better than I did last year—a *lot* better—the Yankees may release me," he said. "I'll be out of baseball and never make it to the big leagues."

"Do you know why you're so intense about that, Honey?" I asked.

He said he didn't.

"There must be some reason. It seems more like an obsession than a drive—as if you think your life will be ruined if you don't make it. Why is making it to the major leagues so important?"

He shook his head. "I don't know," he said.

"Maybe we should pray about it," I said. "Perhaps God could help us get to the bottom of this."

"That's probably a good idea," he said.

So I began praying: "Lord, we don't understand this. But we know You don't want Tim so obsessed about this. Could You show us what's behind this feeling he has?"

At that point I looked up because Tim had begun to cry.

"What is it, Honey?" I asked.

"As you prayed, I remembered something I hadn't thought of for years," he said. "I remembered how proud Mom always was when she came to my games. How she cheered for me. And how much it meant to me whenever she'd say, 'Someday, Tim, you're going to be a major-league pitcher. I just know it.' She even said that to other people."

I looked at Tim and asked, "So if you don't make it to the big leagues, in your mind it will be like burying your mother forever?"

At that, he cried even harder. Then we were both silent for what seemed like hours until I took his hand and sat close beside him. "Can you let that go?" I asked. "If you don't, it's going to haunt you forever."

Very quietly Tim replied, "Yeah. I know I need to let that go."

Tim began to pray through his tears: "Oh Lord, I know what Christine said is true. I need to let this go. And Lord, I also need to let my mom go."

For the first time in the eight years since she died, Tim finally grieved for his mother. I knew he was letting his brother go as well. And we cried together.

CHAPTER SEVEN

The Yankee Doghouse

Tim

I ARRIVED AT THE YANKEES' 1983 MINOR-LEAGUE TRAINING CAMP in Hollywood, Florida, feeling even more uncertain and anxious than I had at my first spring training with the Pirates two years earlier. At least I had met some people in the Pirates' organization after the 1980 amateur draft. And some of them had known me—if not personally, they had at least scouted me enough to want to draft me ahead of hundreds of other promising college and high-school players.

Everything about my first training camp with the Pirates had been incredibly exciting. I was so determined to prove myself in professional competition that I never stopped thinking about baseball long enough to be bothered by my usual awkwardness in unfamiliar situations. All the A-level players had been in pretty much the same situation anyway. We were all new.

But from the first day, the Yankees' camp felt different. Working out with the AAA team, I soon realized that most of the other players not only knew each other, but many of them had also developed close friendships during previous years in AA and A ball. I felt like an outsider who had to work for acceptance off the field as well as on.

Even the New York management knew little or nothing about me. They had my statistics from Buffalo (which sure wasn't much comfort to me), but not even the coaching staff knew what to expect from me, which meant I was under constant and close scrutiny. At least I felt that way.

Maybe the added pressure helped my concentration. I worked hard that spring to try to convince the Yankees that I had a future in the organization. And it paid off. While the AAA competition was stiffer and the batters were tougher than any I had ever faced, I turned in one good performance after another. Since I had struggled so much the previous season in Buffalo, my strong showing in camp may have surprised the Yankees. I know it surprised me.

As happy as I was to be doing so well against hitters only one step from the big leagues, I couldn't shake my bad memories from the previous season. I kept thinking, *I'm not really this good.* I fully expected to be sent down to the AA club when the big-league club broke camp and headed north to start the major-league season.

There's a domino effect every year at the end of spring training. The last few players cut from a team's major-league roster get sent over to the minor-league camp. To make room on the AAA roster, a number of players who spent the spring working with that squad get moved down to AA, and some of the AA guys are, in turn, demoted to A.

But this time, I wasn't one of the dominoes. Camp ended, and I got my assignment. The Yankees were sending me to Columbus, Ohio, to pitch for their AAA club in the International League.

As excited as I was by my unexpected arrival at the top level of the minor leagues, I was also more than a little scared. I kept telling myself, *If you did it in spring training, you can do it in Columbus.* But my doubts were always whispering in my other ear, *Who are you kidding? Remember Buffalo? That was just AA. This is AAA. You don't belong here!*

Christine

TIM AND I TALKED OFTEN ABOUT HIS CONFIDENCE LEVEL. I WORRIED that his doubts were going to affect his performance. I knew competition at the AAA level was so intense that Tim needed any edge he could get. So I tried to bolster his feelings by reminding him how well he had pitched all spring. In my mind, he certainly deserved to make the Columbus team. I just wished he could be happy with the surprise assignment.

In addition to being one phone call away from his major-league goal, there were other reasons to feel good about the new season. Columbus was a lot closer to home than any other city Tim had played for. The team facilities were a huge step up from the lower ranks of the minor leagues—a nice ballpark and better equipment. Perhaps the biggest difference for Tim was that it meant no more grueling, all-night bus trips. AAA teams flew to their away games.

Financially, the promotion made little difference. We had made $1,000 a month for the five-month season in Buffalo. In Columbus, Tim got $1,200 a month—just enough to afford a furnished studio apartment. That meant I didn't have to spend our first couple of weeks in town visiting secondhand stores and searching out neighborhood yard sales before we could set up housekeeping.

The AAA players tended to be a little older, and more of them were married. I began to build friendships with several players' wives; some of us even started an exercise class together. Among these women, I began to sense yet another real difference from previous seasons. There was an air of camaraderie born of years of shared experience and hardships. But along with a new sense of anticipation—the feeling that "we've almost made it"—there was also an underlying and largely unspoken sense of competition. The closer you got to the top, the more you wanted to get there. The stakes were certainly higher at the AAA level. And while I think most of the wives, like most of the players, wished their friends well, we all knew there are only so many positions on a big-league roster. If only one player was called up, we each wanted it to be our husband.

Despite the potential for jealousy and competitive tension, most baseball players' wives, especially in the minor leagues, learned to depend on each other. At most, we knew we would be spending five months at a time in any one town. We had no other friends there and little incentive to try to put down roots. Other wives were our only prospect for developing lasting relationships, the only social and support group we had. So we worked at developing friendships quickly and making our unusual relationships work.

For the first time in his career, Tim tried to make the adjustment from starting pitcher to the bullpen (relief pitching). As one of the low men on the pitching staff, Tim was assigned the role of long reliever. That meant that every time a starting pitcher struggled early in a game, Tim would begin warming up and wait for the call to pitch. But whenever a starter made it to the middle innings or later, a setup pitcher and other relievers would go into the game. So Tim wasn't pitching many innings, which frustrated him.

One day, however, Tim came home especially excited. He announced that he had been picked to join the major-league team the next week as the Yankees played an exhibition game against their AA club in Nashville. Tim explained that since such off-day exhibitions are essentially publicity promotions to boost minor-league attendance and morale, big-league teams seldom want to put any wear and tear on their own pitchers. So they call on some of their minor-league prospects to pitch for the big club.

Tim was one of the lucky ones chosen for the trip. It was going to be his first chance to play with major leaguers and make an impression on the Yankees' top people. I could tell he was excited, and I was excited for him.

Tim

FOR YANKEE PLAYERS, THE GAME IN NASHVILLE WAS A MEANINGLESS exhibition. I knew there wasn't one of them who would not rather have had the day off. But that didn't diminish the thrill I felt putting on an actual big-league uniform.

Any delusions of grandeur I might have had were diminished somewhat, however, as I donned those historic pinstripes for the first time in a *shower*. The visiting team's dressing room at the Nashville Sounds' ballpark was about par for a AA facility. While it was far better than the public-school classroom back in Alexandria two years earlier, there was not enough room for a full roster of big leaguers accustomed to first-class accommodations. So I was relegated to the showers to get dressed. I hung what I could on a couple of hooks, but I had to leave the rest of my street clothes and equipment on the shower-room floor.

I didn't mind, though, because for the first time in my life, I was playing for a major-league baseball team. Well, at least I was *warming up* with them before the game. I didn't really expect to play once I saw I was one of three minor-league pitchers they had brought in. *Just being here is enough*, I told myself. It was, indeed, a thrill to be on the same field, in the same dugout, with people like Dave Winfield, Lou Pinella, Chris Chambliss, Willie Randolph, Goose Gossage, and, of course, the fiery and contro-versial Yankee manager, Billy Martin.

The Nashville fans didn't get much of a show that night. Even with minor-league pitching and most of the Yankee subs getting prime playing time, the big leaguers had an easy outing, taking a 5-0 lead into the ninth.

Since the Yankees were going to give one of their own pitch-ers, Rudy May, a chance for a little work to finish out the game, and because I had been a long reliever in Columbus, I knew I wouldn't be called on in the bottom of the last inning. I began thinking about my clothes back in the shower room, and I was eager to get them out of there before the big-league guys started showering. That meant I needed to be dressed and out of the way as soon as possible—the sooner the better, I figured. I didn't want to get in anyone's way.

Without saying anything to anyone, I slipped out of the dugout during the bottom of the ninth and made my way back into the empty clubhouse. I quickly peeled off my uniform, moved my pile of clothes to the floor in the middle of the locker room, where they would stay dry, and took a hurried shower. I was still toweling off when I heard someone coming down the runway outside the dressing room calling, "Burke! You in here?"

"Yeah," I responded before I could see who it was.

"Get out here and warm up fast," barked Sammy Ellis, the Yankee pitching coach, as he walked through the door. "Billy wants you to pitch the last inn . . ."

He stopped in midsentence, and his mouth dropped open in shock when he saw me standing there dripping wet, towel in hand.

"Uh, well, I guess you can't do it now," he said, turning on his heel and heading back out to the field, muttering about what he was going to tell Billy.

That last inning seemed like the longest inning of my life. I sat alone in the locker room, dressed in my street clothes, convinced I was the world's biggest idiot. Without a doubt, I had just made the dumbest move of my entire athletic career. No, of my entire life.

I had come to Nashville hoping for a chance to make an impression. When Billy Martin came into the clubhouse after the game, he let me know just what kind of impression I had made. A public hanging, stark naked, on the pitcher's mound in Yankee Stadium would have been more merciful and less humiliating than the x-rated tongue-lashing the tough Yankee manager gave me in that crowded locker room.

I desperately wished I could explain the thinking that had made my behavior seem so reasonable at the time. But it already seemed so boneheaded to me that I couldn't imagine how I could explain it, short of claiming complete and total brain cramp. All I could do was acknowledge my utter and colossal stupidity, say "I'm sorry," and stand there absorbing Billy's tirade.

When he finally ran out of steam and the brightest colors began to fade from his extensive vocabulary, Billy suddenly stopped shouting and stormed off to the far side of the locker room, leaving me wishing there were a back way out. At that moment, I'd rather have been carried out in a pinstriped coffin than have to walk out and climb on the Yankees' team bus.

That's about the time Yankees' owner George Steinbrenner strode into the locker room. He and Billy began an animated exchange, with too many dark looks cast my way for me not to know who and what they were talking about. So much for my future with the Yankees.

To my relief, Mr. Steinbrenner left without coming over and adding to my humiliation. And before the team left the ballpark, Billy Martin, to his credit, came back over and said, "Hey, don't worry about it. Just go back to Columbus and do your best to have a good year. And try to forget tonight, kid."

While I appreciated the conciliatory gesture, I knew I'd never forget that night. And I doubted the Yankees would, either.

To make matters worse, I never got the chance to have a good year in Columbus. I experienced more and more difficulty getting my arm loosened up. Every time I pitched, it took longer to really warm up. Soon my shoulder began to hurt. The diagnosis: tendinitis. The prescription: rest. So I went on the disabled list (DL).

Looking back, I think the problem resulted from my unfamiliar relief role. Any time the call came down to the bullpen early in a game, I tried to warm up fast in order to be ready when needed. But if the starter pitched his way out of the jam, I sat down again, only to be up throwing hard again an inning or so later. I wasn't getting into many games, but I was putting an unaccustomed strain on my arm by warming up fast and hard night after night.

A couple of days after I went on the DL, the manager called me to his office and told me I was being demoted to the AA team in Nashville. He said the trainer didn't think my injury would take too long to heal, but they had to make room on the roster for a rookie player the big club was sending down for a little more seasoning. So a young first baseman named Don Mattingly made his last trip down to the minors to sharpen his hitting skills in Columbus. And I went home to tell Christine she would have to pack up and move us to Nashville.

CHAPTER EIGHT

Out of Baseball?

Christine
♥♥♥♥♥

I TRIED TO PUT A GOOD FACE ON FOR TIM'S SAKE. BUT I SANK TO the verge of depression after he flew to Nashville to join his new team, leaving me to break the lease we signed just weeks before, move out of our apartment, and transfer our small but growing stockpile of personal belongings to our second hometown of the season.

Saying sudden good-byes to my new friends was awkward and hard. Thinking about starting over with a new group of wives in Nashville seemed even worse.

Moving at least three or four times a year, sometimes on a few days' notice, can get old fast. But at least until this point in Tim's career, every move had seemed like a step in the right direction. For me, the biggest plus about Columbus had been realizing we were only one last move from the big leagues. Now, a few short weeks later, we were moving *down* the ladder.

Theoretically, if Tim did well in Nashville, he could be called up to Columbus again before the season was over. But what if he didn't do better? What about next year? How long would he bounce around in the minor leagues? I knew wives of players who had played six, eight, even ten years of minor-league ball. How many moves would we make before Tim made it or decided he wouldn't make it?

The good news about the move to Nashville was that Tim would be a starter again. The coaches promised to work him into their rotation as soon as his shoulder healed—which took only a couple of weeks. The bad news was that while Tim's shoulder was fine, his pitching wasn't.

He quickly went 0-3 with an additional poor outing resulting in a no-decision. I tried to keep his spirits up, reminding him that he had been hurt and hadn't pitched regularly since spring training, that he just needed a little time. But I knew he was remembering Buffalo and feeling the pressure of struggling in AA ball for the second year in a row. With each loss, I could sense the tide of discouragement rising higher and higher.

Tim

I STARTED MY NEXT GAME AT HOME IN NASHVILLE AGAINST THE Chattanooga Lookouts. And while I didn't want to magnify the importance of the start and psych myself out, I couldn't help but sense that the pressure was building. We had a good team, so I felt I was letting my teammates down. And since none of them knew me, I wanted desperately to prove I was better than I'd shown since arriving from Columbus.

Until then, the pressure I felt during my professional career had come almost entirely from within—it was pressure I put on myself. But I also knew that was going to change soon if I didn't begin to turn my season around. If I had learned anything about the Yankees' organization during my few short months with them, it was their emphasis on winning—from the top of the organization all the way down. Not that the Pirates' minor-league clubs didn't want to win. But there was an entirely different feel in the Yankees' farm system. The urgency to win seemed almost tangible. There was no doubt I needed to begin winning, and soon, or I would be gone—perhaps out of baseball entirely.

I tried to put all that out of my mind as I walked to the mound to warm up in the top of the first inning. When Chattanooga's leadoff man stepped into the box, I focused all my attention on my catcher, mentally checking his sign and his target against what I remembered from our scouting report on the Lookouts.

First pitch. Strike one. On the next pitch, however, he rocketed a single into right field. I told myself, *One man doesn't matter.* But then I walked the second hitter. The next batter smashed a double off the wall, and suddenly I trailed 2-0. The number four man hit a shot my left-fielder hauled down on the run, but I knew I wasn't fooling anyone. One out. The next Lookout hitter launched a hanging curve out of the yard, and the score was 4-0, Chattanooga.

At that point, our pitching coach, Hoyt Wilhelm, ambled lazily out to the mound. I would have been ready to hit the showers, but I'd blown up so fast that the long relief man in the bullpen wasn't warmed up yet. So all Hoyt could do was offer a little clichéd encouragement in his slow southern drawl: "Don't worry, kid. You're okay. Just get the next guy. Take your time. Settle down. This ain't nuthin'. "

Yeah, right, I thought. *Nuthin' but my career.*

The next hitter singled. *A double play here could end the inning and stop the bleeding.* Another double off the wall, and one more Lookout player scored.

This time, the skipper approached the mound already signaling the bullpen. When I handed him the ball, it was all I could do to keep from sprinting off the field. I had to force myself to walk to the dugout with my eyes straight ahead. I sat alone at the end of the bench and watched my replacement get the final two outs of the inning.

That game marked the worst start of my baseball career. One-third of an inning pitched. Five earned runs. I couldn't remember seeing any professional pitcher do worse.

As my teammates finally walked off the field into the dugout, I turned and looked up into the stands where I knew Christine was sitting. She was looking my way, so I motioned toward the clubhouse with my head and mouthed the words, "Let's go!" Hoping she understood, I walked out of the dugout and back down the runway under the stands.

I wanted so badly to get out of the ballpark, I didn't even bother to shower.

Christine

I WAS SITTING IN THE STANDS WITH SOME OF THE OTHER WIVES THAT night, trying not to let my own nervousness show before the game started. I knew how much Tim wanted a good outing to prove himself to his Nashville teammates. But I was more concerned he would have a good game and prove something to himself. I knew his confidence had taken some serious blows.

After the first two runs scored, my heart sank, and I knew he was in trouble. When he motioned toward the clubhouse and left the dugout, I was more than ready to go. He walked out through the players' gate just moments after I got there. He looked so defeated that I didn't know what to say, so I just gave him a hug, and we trudged to the car in silence.

Later that evening, alone in our tiny studio apartment, Tim voiced for the first time his growing fear. "The way this season has gone," he said, "after this game tonight, I think there's a strong chance I'll be released. That could mean I'll be out of baseball for good."

I thought for a minute, wondering what to say. Then it came to me. "You know, Tim," I told him, "maybe we need to turn your career over to the Lord. We gave our lives to Him, but we never specifically gave Him your baseball career."

"You know," Tim responded without hesitation, "that's a good idea."

So the two of us got down on our knees by our little kitchen table and held hands. We were both crying as Tim prayed first: "Lord, I never even thought about giving You my career. I know I gave You my life, but I guess I never thought about You caring about this stuff. But if I'm holding on to baseball too much, if I want it too much, and it's not what You want for me, help me let it go. I want You to know that I want what You want for our lives. And I won't fight You on this. If You want me to keep going, I'll keep fighting to make it. But if You want me somewhere else, You know what is best."

Then it was my turn to pray, and I said, "Lord this is something Tim has wanted so badly—since he was a little boy. If there's any way he can, if You will give him the strength and the opportunity to do that, he will give it his all. But if it's not Your will for us to stay in baseball, please show us what You have next for our lives."

Then Tim added, "One more thing, Lord. If You want me out

of baseball, could You make it quick? And if You want me in baseball, help us know that soon, too. Our hearts are hurting so, and we can't go on like this much longer."

When we finished, we still had no idea what lay ahead, but we had a new, definite sense of peace.

Tim

I WASN'T CUT BEFORE MY NEXT START, AND I PITCHED WELL ENOUGH to earn my first Nashville win. The following start, I won number two. Then I won again and again. I was on a roll! In fact, I didn't lose another game all season, finishing the 1983 season with a 12-4 record.

Some skeptics might say it was all a coincidence, that I was destined to finish with a great season. But Christine and I were convinced it never would have happened if we hadn't committed my career to the Lord.

I don't want to give the impression that because I did that, God had somehow guaranteed my baseball success. He didn't give me mastery over some great new go-to pitch no one could hit. He didn't magically speed up my fastball or slow down the opposing hitters' swings.

But several beneficial things did happen as a result of committing my career to the Lord. From that day on, I knew I had to concern myself only with my own effort and then trust the Lord with the results. If those results were good, it would be great; if they were bad, I would still believe He wasn't going to make His first mistake with me.

If God was ultimately in charge of my career as well as my life, I didn't have to walk out on the mound worrying what the front office was thinking. The past could be forgotten and forgiven. Nor did I have to worry about what might happen as a result of my performance, because God was in charge of my future whether it was in baseball or not.

With that attitude, the gut-wrenching pressure I had felt all season suddenly disappeared. I felt a peace and a freedom I never felt before. All I had to do was give my best, and that's what I did. Even the fact that I pitched so little the first couple months of the season paid off, as I felt fresh and strong all the way into the league playoffs.

The season ended, and Christine and I moved to San Diego where I'd landed an off-season construction job, confident my time in baseball had not run out. What we didn't know was that my career was about to take a very important and unexpected turn.

Christine
♥♥♥♥♥

ONE DECEMBER DAY, ABOUT THE TIME OF THE MAJOR-LEAGUES' annual winter meetings, Tim and I were sitting on the couch of our San Diego apartment when the phone rang. Tim answered the call.

I could tell from his expression that something was up. Mostly he listened. "When?" I heard him ask. "Who for?" And finally, just before he hung up, "Thanks for calling."

When he turned to look at me, a big smile filled his face. "We've been traded again," he announced.

"To what team?"

"The Montreal Expos."

"Is that good?"

"I think it's great!"

Tim had always preferred the National League. More than anything, he was happy to be out of the Yankees' organization. After ticking off Billy Martin and George Steinbrenner in Nashville, he was worried that he would be blackballed forever. Now he'd have a fresh start in a new organization.

Under other circumstances, I might not have been so happy about the Yankees' lack of faith in my husband. But this trade to the Expos seemed like a godsend. And Tim acted as if he had been given a whole new life.

He certainly pitched like it in 1984 spring training, starting strong and pitching consistently enough to make the Expos'

AAA team in Indianapolis. It was the closest we'd been yet to Nebraska.

In April, when the Expos' minor leaguers finally broke training camp in Florida, Tim and I prepared for our annual migration north by packing everything we owned into our little car's back seat, trunk, and a rented cartop carrier. My plan was to deliver Tim to the Expos' spring training grounds, where he would join his Indianapolis teammates and catch a bus to the airport for their flight north (and the opening of the American Association season the following day). Meanwhile, I would hit the road for Indianapolis and begin the familiar search for affordable (meaning *cheap*) housing.

On our way to training camp to rendezvous with the team, I suddenly saw a movement in the rearview mirror and screamed. Flying out behind us as we raced down Interstate 95 was a stream of the belongings we had carefully packed in the cartop carrier we apparently forgot to latch. I had no idea how long we had been scattering underwear behind us. I shouted "Our things!" and hit the brakes, swerving to a stop on the shoulder.

Tim jumped out and raced back along the highway, dodging in and out of traffic in a desperate and dangerous attempt to retrieve our clothing as it swirled and tumbled along the freeway in the windy wake of passing cars and trucks.

"Forget it, Tim! Come back!" I yelled. It just wasn't worth it. I knew I would never get the tire marks out of my nice silk blouse anyway. But Tim kept running and snatching whatever he could get to before he finally turned and headed back toward me and the car.

In retrospect, that scene of my husband sprinting back and forth across an interstate highway to retrieve a few "precious" belongings seems laughable. But at the time, it seemed almost a tragedy. It certainly underscored the state of our lives at the time—transient, with pitifully little to show for two years of marriage. Salvaging what we could in what time we had. And on the road again.

CHAPTER NINE

Another Chance

Tim

FOR THE SECOND YEAR IN A ROW, I BEGAN THE SEASON 0-4. BUT IN 1984 at Indianapolis, unlike the year before, I didn't think I was pitching that poorly. I just wasn't pitching quite well enough to win.

A couple of days after my fourth loss, I was going through my normal workout, just throwing on the side, when Indianapolis manager Buck Rodgers sauntered up beside me. "Hey, Burke," he said, "come on over to the bullpen with me. I've got an idea I think can help you."

Perhaps the biggest reason I was excited I had been assigned to Indianapolis was Buck Rodgers. He had impressed me during spring training, and everything I had heard about his knowledge of baseball seemed true. He definitely knew the game inside and out. And like a lot of former major-league catchers, he was a great pitching coach.

Buck had been watching me. He thought my easygoing, laid-back personality carried over onto the field. "What I think you need," he said as we stood in the bullpen, "is to be more aggressive. And I think what will help you do that is speeding up your delivery."

Never in my life had I heard a coach tell me or any other pitcher to speed up the pitching motion. In fact, most coaches constantly preach just the opposite:

"Slow down."

"Be deliberate."

"Stay in control."

"Stay within yourself." (Whatever that means.)

Normally, I'm not the kind of person who welcomes change.

But I trusted Buck Rodgers. If he wanted me to speed up my delivery, I'd give it a try. By the end of my first day of pitching differently, the quicker rhythm felt surprisingly comfortable.

The next couple of times I threw, Buck watched me and made suggestions. "Whatever feels comfortable is fine," he said. "Just keep up the pace of your motion. And THINK AGGRESSIVE."

The strategy worked. I won my next start. And the next. I found my groove and began putting together a good season. Buck was right. The quicker, more aggressive windup translated into a more aggressive and confident attitude on the mound. I knew I could get hitters out, so I went right after them.

The longer the season wore on and the better I pitched, the more I began to hope that my performance was being noticed throughout the organization. Maybe there was a chance I would be a September call-up and actually spend the last few weeks of the season in Montreal.

One of my friends on the team, a pitcher named Dick Grapenthin, had actually been up to the majors two or three times for short stints. I remember standing in the Indianapolis outfield one day that summer as he expressed frustration over his most recent up-and-down trip to Montreal.

"You know," I said, trying to raise his spirits, "at least you can say you've been there. My whole goal in baseball right now is just to make it to the big leagues. It would fulfill my dream if I made it for just one day!"

Dick smiled at me knowingly. "You think that now," he said, "but once you get there, one day is not enough. You always want more."

While the big leagues remained a distant dream for me that summer, I felt I was slowly getting closer to that goal. I finished the year with a respectable 12-8 record, an ERA of 3.49, and a lot of innings pitched. We won our division of the American Association by about nine games and played Louisville in the post-season playoffs for the league championship.

I was pleased and a little surprised when Buck pulled me aside after I pitched and won the second game of the series by a score of 4-1. "I may want to use you in relief day after tomorrow," he said, "so don't throw on the side that day. I may need you ready to pitch in the game."

That made me feel good. I had pitched relief a time or two during the season when our bullpen was tired. But it was encouraging that Buck would consider using me when the pressure was on in the playoffs. Sure enough, when our pitcher got in trouble later in the game, Buck told me to start loosening up. We were one run down, one out, with Louisville runners on second and third, when Buck made his second trip to the mound and gave me the call.

My heart pounded as I headed onto the field. I had never come in to relieve in a situation like this. I was absolutely pumped.

The first batter I faced was Terry Pendleton. I struck him out. Then the second man made a harmless third out, and I had escaped the jam. Walking back to the dugout, I said to myself, *I think I could like this bullpen business.* I set down the Cardinals in order in the next inning. But what excited me most was Buck's confidence in me; he had turned to me when everything was on the line. And I came through.

Our season ended a couple of days later when Louisville took the series and the league championship. But what disappointed me more than losing the title was packing up my equipment in the visiting team's locker room and hearing that several of my teammates had just been called up to Montreal for the remainder of the National League season.

I was so upset that without stopping to think about it, I did something very uncharacteristic for me. I closed my locker, set my equipment bag on the floor, and walked into Buck's office. I wasn't at all angry with Buck; I knew it wasn't his decision. But after I closed the door behind me, I told him I thought I had pitched as well as anyone on our roster that season. I believed I deserved a call-up. I was not only disappointed, but I was also upset that I had been slighted.

Buck told me that he, too, thought I had earned a shot. But he also pointed out the organization had a lot of factors to consider. The Expos were obviously giving first chance to the other guys because they had already been listed on the big-league club's official 40-man roster. "But," he said, "I think you've got the makings of a good major-league reliever. Go play some winter ball this off-season, Tim, and get a little more experience. You'll get your chance."

That was all I wanted. One chance.

Christine
♥♥♥♥♥

I THINK I WAS MORE UPSET THAN TIM WHEN HE WASN'T CALLED UP. He had played well all season long and had worked so hard. I understood why the politics of baseball drove the wives crazy. I had a hard time not being resentful.

In October, we flew to Santo Domingo in the Dominican Republic for Tim's first experience with winter ball—and our first exposure to the Third World.

At first it seemed both exciting and scary to be alone in a foreign culture where we didn't even speak the language. But it was also a stretching experience that opened our eyes to the world. In those few short months, we fell in love with the warmth and charm of the Latin people.

We thought we knew what poverty was during those first years of our marriage. But that was poverty by American standards. It was nothing compared to the hunger and suffering we saw every day within blocks of the little hotel where we lived. The $2,000 a month Tim earned playing on the team Felipe Alou managed was several times the average *annual* salary of the avid fans who came to cheer at our games and who made us feel so welcome in their country.

Tim pitched as well as, if not better than, he had in Indianapolis. So all in all, our experience with winter baseball was extremely positive.

Not that we didn't have some disappointments during that off-season. We had been talking for a couple of years about starting a family. I wished I had owned stock in one of the early pregnancy test companies, because I bought a kit every month. *Are we or aren't we?* It was an emotional roller coaster. And every month we failed to get pregnant, I became more and more discouraged.

But the two biggest letdowns that winter came in December. When the new 40-man rosters came out for the annual major-league meetings, Tim didn't make the Expos' list. Then, shortly after that, the leagues conducted their annual minor-league draft (in which unprotected players could be drafted by any organization willing to pay a nominal fee and assign them to a roster level one step higher than their current status). No one drafted Tim. That meant that despite his great showing in Indianapolis and all his years of hard work, there wasn't a single organization in baseball that thought enough of his prospects to give him a shot at the majors. That was a severe blow to Tim's confidence.

Not until we returned to Omaha from the Dominican Republic in late January 1985 did we receive some good news. Tim at least got an invitation from the Expos to attend their major-league training camp in West Palm Beach the next month. And since Buck Rodgers had been named the Expos' manager during the off-season, Tim figured he would get a fair chance to pitch a few times and make a good impression.

As always, I went to Florida with Tim in February. With the extra money we made during winter ball, we could afford a little nicer apartment than we had in the past, which meant there was more room for the cockroaches to run around. But we tried to be grateful for small blessings.

What really mattered was that Tim not only got a chance to pitch, but Buck even scheduled him as the second pitcher to work in the opening game of the spring training season against the Atlanta Braves—a game telecast nationally on superstation WTBS.

Tim pitched three innings that day as I sat in the stands cheering. He didn't allow a run and made two key defensive plays. I was never more excited for him.

Tim

I CONTINUED TO PITCH WELL IN SPRING TRAINING GAMES AND MADE the first cut. The following week, I made the second cut.

Every Monday was payday, the day the Expos gave another week's meal money to each player still in camp. That meant that every Sunday was D-day—the day players learned whether they were being released or sent over to the minor-league camp.

Meal money was the only pay most of us ever received during spring training. And major-league meal money—around $1,600 a month at that time—amounted to more per month than I ever made playing four years of minor-league ball. So those meal checks were almost as important to Christine and me as knowing that I had stuck with the team for another week.

What I didn't learn until years later was that Buck Rodgers was being pressured every week to send me over to the minor-league camp. Every weekend, the new Expos' general manager, Murray Cook, would say to Buck, "We need to pare down the roster. Isn't it about time we cut Burke?" And each weekend, Buck would shake his head and say, "No, not yet. I'd like to give him another outing or two before we do that."

Every three or four days, Buck handed me the baseball and sent me to the mound. And week after week, I pitched the best ball of my life. I posted more innings than any other pitcher in camp, and I only gave up one earned run all spring. So when a couple of veterans developed arm trouble in late March, I began to think I had a legitimate shot at making the Expos' roster.

By the last week of spring training, eleven pitchers remained. We all knew only ten would be going north for opening day. The mathematics were simple. And I knew that the final spot on the pitching staff was now a choice between me and one other guy. I just happened to be in the clubhouse getting dressed the morning the other guy was called into Buck's office. When he walked out a few minutes later, the look on his face told me all I needed to know. I had made the team!

Of course, somebody would have to tell me officially. Until then, I needed to keep my euphoria under control. I had to at least *act* cool.

But a few minutes later, when one of the clubhouse guys stuck his head around a corner to say, "Burke, Buck wants to see you in his office," I started grinning so wide it hurt. I knew I needed to keep my cool, so I quickly walked over to the clubhouse gum rack and grabbed enough Bazooka to make a huge wad. I figured that if I kept my mouth busy chewing gum, maybe I could walk into Buck's office without grinning like a fool.

I strolled in and settled into a chair in front of his desk. Buck sat there for a few moments, shuffling papers and taking his time. I had been around him long enough to know he was enjoying his attempt to create a little suspense. Buck had always let me know he liked and respected me, and he was such a genuinely nice man that I understood he was getting a real kick from anticipating giving me the good news.

I tried to maintain my air of nonchalance as I waited for him to say something. Finally, he looked up at me and grinned. "Congratulations!" he said. "We've decided to take you north with us, Tim. You've made the club."

I couldn't hold back the smile any longer.

I thanked him for giving me the chance. He told me I deserved it; I'd pitched well all spring, and he wanted to pitch me in one more game before we left Florida. I thanked him again and fought back the tears of joy.

I guess I wasn't as cool as I thought I was, because the next day, the newspaper quoted Buck as saying, "Tim Burke walked into my office—and floated out."

I felt as if I *were* floating as I left his office with one thought in mind: *I can't wait to tell Christine!*

CHAPTER TEN

Life in the Big Leagues

Christine
♥♥♥♥♥

I RETURNED HOME FROM THE GROCERY STORE THAT DAY TO FIND A half-dozen notes plastered all over the door of our tiny apartment. Since we couldn't afford our own phone, Tim had called and left several messages with the apartment manager. Every note said the same thing: "Pick up Tim at ballpark."

Obviously, something big was up. It had to be the final cut. Camp was almost over, and Tim had been expecting a decision any day.

I rushed out to the car and headed for West Palm Beach Municipal Stadium, the Expos' training facility. My mind raced with thoughts like *What if Tim's been cut? He'll be devastated. What am I going to say? Surely they wouldn't cut him; he's had a great spring.* But trying to convince myself was a losing battle.

Long before I reached the training camp, my negative thinking had me bracing myself for the news and trying to figure out how in the world I was going to bolster my husband's shattered spirits. The pain I felt for him made me sick, angry, and on the verge of tears.

Tim was waiting for me as I pulled into the players' parking lot. Watching him walk toward the car, I could tell he was trying hard to hold his emotions in check. *Poor guy!* I thought. *What am I going to say?*

He slid into the passenger's seat and leaned back against the headrest without saying anything. "Oh, Honey," I said, "what happened today?"

Without a trace of expression or emotion in his voice, he softly replied, "I made the team."

"Oh, Honey! I'm so sorry. How did . . ." The words finally

registered, and I screamed, "What did you say?"

"I made the team." He was grinning now. "We're going to Montreal."

I screamed again and threw my arms around him for a giant hug. He told me all about the day as we drove straight to a nearby mall, found a couple of pay phones, and began making calls all over the country to report the news. Tim used one phone to talk to all his family and friends, while I took the next one to call mine. "Hi! It's Christine! Tim made the team!" I announced again and again. "We're going to Montreal!"

Actually, Tim wasn't going directly to Montreal. The team was flying from Florida to Cincinnati to open the season. I would pack our belongings into our car and drive north to Canada for yet another season in yet another city. But it was a major-league city at last!

Tim

BEGINNING THE SEASON, I WOULD BE LOW MAN ON THE EXPOS' pitching staff totem pole. I knew I would be relegated to long relief and probably pitch very little. But none of that mattered because I'd made the team! I was so awed by that fact that I could hardly sleep the night before opening day.

I sat in my Cincinnati hotel room watching the local evening news and then a big special on the Reds and their prospects for the '85 season. Opening day of baseball season is always a big event in Cincinnati, the traditional site of the first game of the National League season. The entire city celebrates. The next day promised added excitement because Cincinnati's favorite son, Pete Rose, was returning for his first game as the Reds' player-manager.

As I watched the TV newscasts and the features on Pete Rose and his 1985 squad, I kept marveling, *I'm in their league now. That's the team we're playing against tomorrow.* I felt I should pinch myself. But I couldn't have been dreaming because I was far too excited to sleep.

April 8, 1985. The weather report that morning looked promising—for hockey. The TV weatherman predicted snow flurries for the afternoon. But I didn't care. I couldn't wait to head for the ballpark.

Despite the cold, the opening-day crowd began filling up Riverfront Stadium during batting practice. Cincinnati fans care about baseball, and their team has a storied tradition. Standing out on the field during warm-ups, I could feel the excitement in the ballpark begin to build.

I may have been the most thrilled person in the place. But I can't say I was genuinely nervous until we all stood on the field for the national anthem and I thought, *Here we go. This is really it. What's going to happen now? I've worked my whole life to get to this point. Now here I am.*

I wished Christine could be in the stands to share the moment with me. And Dad and my stepmom, Carol. They had traveled half the country to watch most of my college baseball games. They and my sister, Terri, would have gotten a big kick out of seeing my first major-league game.

I thought, too, about my brother playing catch with me when I was little and telling my parents, "Tim could be a professional athlete when he grows up." I remembered all those times my mom had proclaimed her faith in me by telling me, "One day you'll be a big-league pitcher, Tim." Fighting back tears, I told myself, *I would give almost anything if Dick and Mom could see me standing out on this field.* Opening day. The Montreal Expos and the Cincinnati Reds. *They would have been so proud.*

I also realized the truth of what my friend Dick Grapenthin had tried to tell me the summer before. As excited as I was to be on the field that day for my first major-league game, one day, one game, was no longer enough. *I can't blow this opportunity. I want to stay in the majors.*

Finally, the game began—and I was still there, wearing a big-league uniform in a big-league ballpark, on the same field with guys like Andre Dawson, Tim Raines, Tony Perez, and Pete Rose. It just didn't seem real. It was beyond and better than any dream.

By the third inning, the skies opened up and the flurries became so thick that the umpiring crew called a snow delay. The grounds crew rolled a tarp out over the infield, and the players retreated to the warmth of the clubhouse. As the team's long reliever, I nervously watched our starting pitcher, Steve Rogers, for any sign that his arm was tightening up during the wait. But when Buck went over to find out how he felt, Steve shrugged off the concern and said he'd be fine. So I relaxed.

Play resumed a half hour later, and Steve pitched until the snow came down and delayed the game again, much to the displeasure of 56,000 baseball-hungry Reds' fans. No sooner had I found a seat in the clubhouse again than Buck walked over to me and said, "You're the pitcher when we go back out there."

For the next 45 minutes, there was absolutely nothing I could do but sit in the locker room getting more and more nervous. My major-league debut. Opening day. In front of all those hostile fans.

The flurries finally stopped. We returned to the field, and I walked to the mound to warm up, pretending this was just another baseball game and trying desperately to concentrate completely on my catcher's target. My knees shook. My stomach started a tumbling routine deserving at least a 9.9 from any Olympic gymnastics judge. And in spite of a wind chill factor that would have made a penguin smile, my hands were clammy with sweat.

I inherited a runner on first with two outs and a no-ball, two-strike count on Reds' batter Cesar Cedeño. I took a slow, deep breath in a futile attempt to calm my nerves as I took the sign, checked the runner at first, and made my first major-league pitch. It was a fastball, high and away. The runner at first took off with the pitch, so my catcher, Mike Fitzgerald, came out of his crouch and rifled a perfect throw to second to nail the runner. One pitch. One out. Inning over. I was walking toward the dugout feeling as if the weight of the world had just been lifted off my shoulders. *If I never get another batter,* I figured, *at least I can say I got one out in the major leagues.*

In the bottom of the next inning, I went back out to the mound to face Cedeño again. He promptly tripled off the wall— my first big-league hit allowed. Pete Rose followed with a single, and I had suddenly given up my first RBI (run batted in). I thought, *At least I can say it was to a baseball legend like Pete*

Rose. Then I struck out Nick Esasky (a much better "first") and went on to finish the inning without further damage.

The following inning, I walked one and gave up one hit before retiring the side and leaving the game. I had given up three hits and one run in two and a third innings. While it hadn't been a great performance, I considered it at least satisfactory. Best of all, I got my big, first, crucial appearance out of the way on opening day. And I promised myself, *If I live to be a hundred, I don't ever want to feel that nervous again.*

Christine
♥♥♥♥♥

I SPENT THE AFTERNOON OF OPENING DAY ON THE ROAD, DRIVING north and punching buttons on my car radio in a futile search for a station carrying the Reds-Expos game. When I finally caught a sports report giving the final score—Reds 5, Expos 2—I hoped Tim hadn't been the losing pitcher.

I was caravaning to Canada with another Expos' pitcher's wife, Nancy Hesketh. When we stopped to spend the night at her mom's house, Tim called with a full report. He sounded so uncharacteristically excited, I wished I could have been there in Cincinnati.

I did make the Expos' home opener in Montreal a few days later, but the baseball game is not what I remember most.

Accustomed as we were to a tight budget, we had been so frugal with our major-league meal money in spring training that we actually had a little saved by the time we left Florida. "Why don't you buy yourself a nice, new coat?" Tim suggested. "It's still going to be cold in Montreal."

I didn't own a good coat, so I gladly went out and bought myself an expensive (by my standards), down-filled ski jacket. I went to Montreal's home opener feeling very stylish and chic—until, that is, I walked into the wives' section at the stadium. I never saw so much mink in one place in my life! One look and it was obvious: I was the rookie's wife.

But like Tim, I was excited just to be there. I was even more excited for Tim, and I wanted to do something memorable to celebrate. Tim always loved dogs, so when he returned from his first extended road trip with the Expos and walked through the door of our new apartment, I greeted him with a tiny cocker spaniel puppy.

We named him Slider because I believed that was the pitch that got Tim to the major leagues. And as long as we had Slider, he reminded us of the excitement we shared during Tim's first season in the National League.

Suddenly we were part of a first-class life-style we weren't accustomed to or prepared for. I remember the first road trip I went on with Tim. (The Expos had a policy allowing wives and families to accompany the team on two road trips per year at the club's expense.) Just flying was a thrill for me. When we got to the team's four-star hotel, we checked in and were walking through the door of our room when I looked around and grabbed Tim's arm in panic. "Someone's stolen our luggage!" I said. I had packed the only nice clothes I owned in my suitcase for this trip to Chicago.

"It's okay, Christine," Tim assured me. "The bellhop took it. They deliver your bags to your room here."

"Oh," I replied in relief, glad no one but Tim was there to witness my naiveté. I was even more glad I hadn't spotted and tackled the bellhop who had picked up our bags in the lobby.

I felt very out of place surrounded daily by the ever present media and the trappings of money. The contract Tim signed called for a major-league minimum salary, $40,000 a season that year. While that didn't begin to compare to the big bucks a lot of his teammates received, it was a fortune compared to the $8,000 he made in AAA ball the year before. For the first time in our married life, we could pay the rent at the first of the month and not worry about stretching the groceries until Tim's next payday.

Tim

I WOULD BE LYING IF I SAID THE MONEY AND THE MAJOR-LEAGUE life-style didn't make an impression on me as well. They did.

I remember boarding our charter flight for my first road trip. I had barely buckled myself into my seat when the Expos' traveling secretary walked back through the plane distributing each player's meal money. Just as he handed me a sealed envelope with my name on the outside, veteran infielder Doug Flynn turned around to watch me open it. "Hey, Rookie," he said with a grin, "remember this is just meal money. It's not your paycheck."

I opened the envelope and quickly thumbed through cash totaling more than any bimonthly paycheck I had received in Indianapolis the year before. I certainly wouldn't have to eat any cheeseburgers with fries unless I wanted to.

I could get used to this real quick, I thought. I just hoped I'd have the chance.

Despite pitching well in my first few outings of long relief, I expected the time could soon come when one of the injured veterans would get well and I would be sent back down to Indianapolis. Not that I didn't feel accepted by my Expos teammates. I just couldn't muster any confidence that I really and truly belonged in the big leagues—until our first trip into Los Angeles that May.

Because I grew up as a Dodger fan, playing in L.A. meant something very special to me. Every summer during high school and college, I spent a week or two visiting relatives in Southern California. I always tried to schedule those trips when the Dodgers were in town. Every night I could, I would go by myself to Dodger Stadium, buy the cheapest ticket I could find, and sit in the upper deck to watch the games and imagine what it would be like to stand on the same mound where great pitchers like Sandy Koufax and Don Drysdale had once stood and pitched in a major-league baseball game.

Bill Gullickson started for the Expos our first night in town. When he pulled a groin muscle in the first inning, our trainers rushed out, checked him over, and he finished the inning. But he couldn't go back out in the bottom of the second. Buck Rodgers gave me the ball, and I walked out onto that historic diamond, my own personal field of dreams, to face the Los Angeles Dodgers for the first time in my career.

Standing on the mound, I looked into the Dodger dugout at all those men in blue. Then I looked up into the upper deck where I always used to sit and thought, *I'm out here. I'm really out here.*

For five innings that night at Dodger Stadium, I pitched shutout baseball, giving up only one hit to the great Los Angeles Dodgers. And when I left the game for a pinch hitter in the seventh, I walked off the field believing for the first time that I belonged in the big leagues and deserved to stay there.

Christine
♥♥♥♥♥

ON MAY 29, TIM GOT A CHANCE TO PITCH IN SAN DIEGO, THIS TIME in front of his entire family. As Tim sprinted from the bullpen to the mound that night, I saw his dad, proudly sporting an Expos cap, reach into his pocket and pull out a small leather pouch. As he took something out of the pouch, he noticed me watching him. "Rolaids?" he offered with a grin.

"Sure. I could use one," I conceded.

Then, with his dad and his wife eating Rolaids, Tim pitched one scoreless inning of relief to earn his first big-league win. Jeff Reardon recorded the final out of the game, and as Tim's personal cheering section went wild, I looked down the row and noticed my father-in-law had tears in his eyes. As he turned his head to hide them, Terri asked him, "What do you think about your son tonight?"

"Well . . . " He was too choked up to respond.

Tim went on to set a club record by becoming the first Expos rookie to go 8-0 at the start of his career before giving up his first major-league loss at the end of August. But what excited Tim just as much as how *well* he pitched was how *much* he was getting to pitch. Though Buck Rodgers began the season using Tim as a long reliever, he soon began using him more and more as the setup man for the Expos' premier closer, Jeff Reardon.

Tim tied a major-league rookie record that year by appearing in 78 games. Because he had been a starter for most of his minor-league career, I worried about the strain on his arm as he sometimes pitched two or three days in a row. But Jeff Reardon became a true friend, taking Tim under his wing and teaching him how a reliever needs to warm up and train to keep his arm in shape, ready to go into a game with only a few minutes' notice.

That may have been why Tim stayed healthy all season, finishing the year with a 9-4 record, eight saves, and a very respectable ERA of 2.39. His 78 game appearances also led the National League for the 1985 season. *Baseball Digest* even named Tim to its All-Rookie team. Tim's entire rookie season was like one long baseball dream come true.

Another dream came true that summer when we were finally able to buy our first house—a townhouse, really. Sometime around the middle of the summer, we decided I should go back to Omaha and look for a place we could live in during the off-season; something small and reasonable, with three bedrooms. Tim gave me a list of what he wanted. I discovered a new development with an unsold lot and a foundation already started. I toured the builder's models and mailed photos to Tim, with arrows pointing out "our lot" and "our foundation." I guess I had pretty much made up "our" mind. Tim gave his okay, and I signed the contract. Our townhouse would be ready when the season ended in October.

As much as I enjoyed the adventure of our new life in Montreal, I began looking forward to the end of the season. I disliked moving so much that it seemed strange to be excited about the prospect of packing and unpacking all our belongings one more time. But this move was different from all the others. We weren't moving into an unknown city in search of the cheapest temporary housing. No more living in basements. No more cramped studio apartments with drab, dingy walls. We were moving into a real house, and it was going to be ours.

I told Tim, "The first thing I'm going to do when we move in is get a nice, big picture. Then I'm going to hammer a nail in our living room wall to hang it on. And if I don't like the way it looks, I'm going to hammer another nail, and another, and another, until I get the picture exactly where I want it. I won't

have to worry about nail holes because it's going to be *our wall!"*
Tim laughed and threatened to hide the hammer.

Tim

FOR THE REST OF MY LIFE, WHEN I THINK OF MY ROOKIE YEAR, I'll always remember four special games. Opening day in the snow at Cincinnati. My first game pitching in Dodger Stadium. That first win pitching in front of my family in San Diego. And the last day of the season in New York.

The crowd filled Shea Stadium for the Mets' final outing, but not because the game mattered. They had come hoping to win one of the big prizes the Mets planned to give away for their annual Fan Appreciation Day. Both teams were out of the pennant race; the game wouldn't affect the final standings. In fact, it was such a meaningless contest that several of the Mets' regulars sat out the game to allow their substitutes and their September call-ups some playing time.

But there was one person in the ballpark that sunny Sunday afternoon for whom the outcome of the game could be very significant. My friend and teammate Jeff Reardon had been battling the Chicago Cubs' Lee Smith all season for the honor of "Rolaids National League Relief Man of the Year." Winning the title would earn Jeff a $50,000 bonus. And since the award was based on saves and ERA, our team statistician did some calculations before the final game and told us exactly what had to happen for Jeff to beat Lee Smith. He needed to pitch two shutout innings and get credit for a save.

Of course, that meant we'd not only have to win the game, but we would also have to be just far enough ahead of the Mets going into the bottom of the eighth inning that Jeff could qualify for an official save. That meant that in my designated role as setup man, I could play a pivotal part in the scenario.

Sure enough, we had a meager one-run lead when Buck Rodgers called the bullpen for me. I doubt there was a fan in Shea Stadium who could have understood the weight I felt on my back as I ran out to the mound to pitch the bottom of the sixth inning in such a meaningless game. Of course, every one of my Expos teammates knew exactly what I had to do because they were all pulling for Jeff to be Reliever of the Year. But I was the one who had to hold the Mets scoreless for the next two innings. Six outs.

I had a terrible time concentrating on pitching to the first hitter. I kept thinking how much I owed Jeff for his friendship and help that season. I thought he was the best reliever in the game; no doubt about it. He had had an incredible year, and he deserved the honor—and the money.

The money. A $50,000 bonus! It was more than my entire year's salary, and it was far more than all the money I had earned in five previous years of playing professional baseball. And it was all riding on my ability to pitch two scoreless innings against the always-dangerous New York Mets.

Fortunately, the Mets' big guns—Keith Hernandez, Gary Carter, and Daryl Strawberry—all were sitting out. I faced three subs in the sixth and set them down one, two, three. One inning to go.

In the bottom of the seventh, as the first Mets hitter stepped into the box to face me, the capacity crowd began to cheer. When I looked over toward the Mets' dugout, I saw why. Daryl Strawberry stood in the on-deck circle, taking his warm-up swings to pinch hit!

After I got the first hitter on a harmless grounder, Strawberry stepped into the box. Always a big, imposing figure at the plate, he had hit well against me the few times I faced him that year. And with a suddenly boisterous crowd rocking the stands, I knew he would like nothing better than to thrill the fans with a long ball. He'd be swinging for the fences.

I threw a slider on the corner that he took for strike one. When I got the ball back, I walked around the mound and took a few deep breaths. On my next pitch, I tried to handcuff him with a fastball inside, but I didn't get it in far enough. He turned on it and absolutely crushed it high and deep to right.

As I whirled to watch that rocket take off, in my mind I could see $50,000 stapled to the ball, heading deep into the stands beyond the right-field fence. But as the ball soared, it also began to hook. And hook. Until it passed maybe five feet to the right of the pole. Foul ball.

Oh, man! I was never more relieved in all my life. I had another chance. I threw my next pitch, a fastball, high and away. Strawberry swung and missed for strike three. I got the next man out, and the inning ended. The rest was up to Jeff, who got the save, the award, and the bonus.

My rookie season in the big leagues had come to a memorable end.

CHAPTER ELEVEN

Old Problems, New Start

Christine
♥♥♥♥♥

WITH TIM'S IMPRESSIVE ROOKIE SEASON AND THE PURCHASE OF OUR first home, 1985 was a milestone year for the Burkes. But not all the memories were good.

One night while Tim was gone on a late-season road trip, I called the Houston hotel where the Expos were staying. It was well after midnight, but I figured Tim would still be up, as he usually was after a night game. The minute Tim answered his phone, I knew he hadn't been asleep. "What are you doing?" I asked.

"Whatdyamean?" he slurred.

"Why do you sound so funny, Tim?" I asked. But I knew. We had had too many conversations like this the first two years I knew Tim.

"What . . . ?"

"You've been drinking, haven't you?"

"Uh . . . I just had a couple beers with a bunch of the guys . . ."

"A couple?" I couldn't believe that. I couldn't believe any of what I was hearing. And I think that's what I screamed at Tim— "*I don't believe this!*"—before I slammed down the phone.

Tim had not been drunk even once in the three years since we became Christians. But just hearing his slurred voice on the phone opened a cesspool of ugly feelings and painful memories dating back to those miserable times in our relationship. Was his drinking problem starting again?

I thought Tim's drinking would kill me back then. I knew I couldn't live through that nightmare a second time. In fact, the very thought of Tim drunk in a Houston hotel room made me physically ill. And I was angrier at my husband than I'd ever been.

That's why, as soon as I'd hung up on Tim, I took the receiver off the hook.

Tim

THE COMBINATION OF CHRISTINE'S CALL AND MY OWN GUILT sobered me up fast. For the next few hours, I tried to call home. All I got was a busy signal.

Finally, at about five in the morning, I got through. Christine answered after a couple of rings. I could tell she was still upset, so I began by telling her how sorry I was, promising it would never happen again, and trying to explain what had happened. There had been a team party, and because I didn't want my new teammates to think I was some kind of stick-in-the-mud, I joined them. I had a couple of beers just to try to fit in, and before I knew it, I was drunk.

At that point, realizing what a lousy Christian example I was to my teammates, I left the party and went alone to my room. That's when Christine called and . . . "I can't tell you how sorry I am. I love you, and I promise it won't ever happen again. Please forgive me and try not to be upset."

I waited for some kind of response. She didn't say anything for a long time. When she did, her voice remained cold and angry.

"Well, I am upset. In fact, I'm so upset right now, I'm not sure I'll meet you in Cincinnati." (She was planning to join me a couple of days later for the last leg of our road trip.) "I'm not even sure," she added, "that I'll be here when you get back."

Then she abruptly hung up and took the phone off the hook again.

Christine

FOR THE NEXT TWO HOURS, I CRIED AND PRAYED, POURING OUT ALL my pain and anger to God, telling Him that if this was what major-league baseball was going to do to Tim, it wasn't worth it. When I finally exhausted myself and was quiet, I felt a clear sense of God speaking softly to my broken heart. It was as if He were saying, *Okay, I understand how hurt you are. But what I want you to do when you talk to Tim again is tell him that you will be here for him, that you will forgive him, and that I already have.*

"You tell him that!" I told God. "I don't think I could, even if I wanted to."

I did finally call Tim back at about 7:00. When he told me again how sorry he was and that it would never happen again, I remembered all the times he had made and broken that same promise before we got married. But I managed to deliver the message I thought God wanted me to deliver.

Through clenched teeth, I told Tim I would try to forgive him, that God already had, and that I had decided I would meet him in Cincinnati after all. When he heard that, Tim began to cry like a baby. My words demolished him.

Not until then was I finally convinced his remorse was truly genuine.

Tim

NEVER IN MY LIFE HAD I FELT LIKE SUCH AN UTTER AND COMPLETE failure. I had failed Christine. I had failed myself. I had failed my teammates by not being the kind of Christian example I wanted to be. I had failed God. I had blown it big-time.

To make matters worse, I suddenly realized it was Sunday morning, and I was scheduled to give my Christian testimony in a morning worship service at a Houston church.

My first thought was, *No way. Not after this. I'll have to cancel. Tell them I'm sick or something.* After the night I had, I could honestly say I felt horrible.

But it was too late. I couldn't cancel now. So I went. I didn't want to. And I would never have found the emotional or spiritual strength to do it if Christine hadn't offered her words of forgiveness. I don't remember exactly what I said in church that morning. But I do remember sitting on the front row of the sanctuary feeling like the world's biggest hypocrite.

As horrible and humiliating as that whole incident was, a number of good things came out of it. It scared me into realizing I couldn't ever drink again, even socially, without running a risk I wasn't willing to take. It humiliated me to realize how I'd failed and hurt God. It showed me how far I had to go yet as a Christian. And it convinced me I needed more spiritual input and help.

That's why I told Christine at season's end that I wanted us both to attend the Professional Athletes Outreach (PAO) conference early in the off-season. PAO is a Christian organization whose purpose is to help professional athletes and their families grow spiritually and deal with the unique circumstances and problems they face in professional sports.

Christine
♥♥♥♥♥

I DIDN'T WANT TO GO. I KNEW THE EPISODE IN HOUSTON HAD REALLY bothered Tim and convinced him he needed help. But I was trying hard to forget what happened, my anger, and the sense of betrayal I felt.

When Tim finally said, "If you believe in our marriage, you'll do this for me," I agreed to go to the conference. It turned out to be a positive experience for both of us—so positive, in fact, that when we got back to Omaha and Tim expressed a desire to talk to the counseling pastor of our church, I quickly agreed to go with him.

Of course, my thinking was that we were going to get help for Tim's drinking problem. I was willing to do that. But on our second counseling visit, Pastor Steve, who had spent most of the session listening to me tell how Tim's drinking had affected our marriage, turned to Tim. "Tell me, Tim," he asked, "what does forgiveness mean to you?"

Tim gave a nice definition that sounded pretty complete and theologically correct. Steve smiled and nodded his approval.

"Now Christine," he said, looking at me, "what does forgiveness mean to you?"

"Well . . . uh . . . what Tim said," I replied.

Steve gave me a little smile. "What does it mean to you to forgive? Tell me in your own words."

"Uh . . . I'm not sure I can," I said. I started squirming, feeling quite embarrassed. I suddenly realized I had been a Christian for three years but didn't really know what forgiveness meant. I wasn't sure I had ever really forgiven anyone.

Steve sensed my embarrassment as he gently said, "One reason forgiveness is such a hard concept for people is that they want to base it on feelings. If you base your forgiveness of Tim or anyone else on feelings, you'll never do it. Think for a minute about someone who has been raped. How could a rape victim ever wake up in the morning and say, 'Today's the day I feel like forgiving the person who raped me'? You could never do that."

"You're right," I responded. "There's no way I will ever wake up and think, *Today I feel like forgiving the guy who broke my neck*. I can't do it. I'll never do it. It's impossible."

Steve explained that it *is* impossible *if* we base forgiveness on feelings. "You have to forgive out of obedience," he said. "Not because you feel like it, but because Jesus asks us to do it [see Matthew 18:21-22]. We do it out of obedience and love for Him."

Then he asked, "Do you think you could ever forgive like that?"

"No," I said. "I honestly don't think I can. I've been hurt too deeply. I'm not even sure I want to forgive some of the people who have hurt me."

"That's your choice," Steve told me. And that's the way we ended our session.

The next week, I spent a long time thinking about everything that had been done to me, reliving my pain and grief. After all that soul searching and spiritual struggle, we went back for our next session. The first thing I said to Steve was, "I want to do it. I want to be forgiving. But I just don't know how. I'm not sure I can."

"Okay," Steve said. And he took a couple of pieces of paper out of his desk—8 1/2 x 11 sheets of white paper that had each been cut into the shape of a cross. He handed one to Tim and the other to me—along with a red pen. "What I want you to do," he said, "is write down on this cross all the things that have been done to you that you haven't forgiven people for. Include all the things you've never forgiven yourself for. And list all the things you've never forgiven God for."

I thought, *I'm going to need a lot bigger cross. Don't you have a giant one?*

"Okay," I said. "I'll do it. But I don't know how I'll be able to forgive." *How do you forgive a father who left you before you were born, who totally abandoned you and never paid a penny of child support, causing your mother to be absent a lot, so that things happened that should never happen to a child? How do you forgive a man whose negligence caused an accident that broke your neck and left a lifelong legacy of pain, so much pain you can't vacuum a floor without hurting? How do you forgive an alcoholic husband who's hurt you so many times? How do you forgive yourself for all the horrible things you've done in a lifetime? How do you forgive God for letting it all happen in the first place?*

I wrote it all down with the red pen Steve said represented the blood Christ shed on the cross for our forgiveness. But the whole time I was thinking, *This isn't going to work. I can't do this.* When I finished, I said to Steve, "I still think it's impossible."

"That's where the grace of God comes in, Christine," he said. "In a minute, we're going to pray and confess these things . . ."

"Out loud?" I interrupted.

"Yes," he said, "because the Bible tells us in the book of James to confess our sins one to another."

"You're not going to tell anyone this stuff, are you?" I was truly ashamed of some of the things on my list.

"No," Steve said. "This is just between you and the Lord. But it's important for you to verbalize it. And when you finish, I want you to conclude your prayer by saying, 'Lord, I'm not capable of forgiveness like this. Only You are. Unless You give me the power and the grace, I'll never be able to forgive these people.' "

That's exactly what I prayed after going completely through my list, front and back. As I finished, I felt an overwhelming sense of God's presence. It was as if He were saying, "Christine, you have no idea how much mercy and forgiveness I have." It was as if He gave me a measure of His forgiveness for others and myself. For the first time in my life, I felt truly and completely accepted and loved.

All my life, I had been a harsh, hurt, mean, and bitter person inside. Sure, I was fun and bubbly on the outside, but I was screaming and dying on the inside. All my life, I had been a prisoner of unforgiveness. Now I had learned how to be free!

My life was changed forever that day, and so was our marriage. It was as if we had a fresh, new start.

We both felt it.

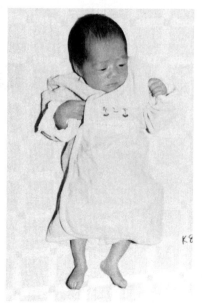

(overleaf) Tim holds Stephanie,
reaching for the mike at 18 months old,
during a spring training pregame event in 1989.
(photo © by E.A. Kennedy III, *West Palm Beach Post*)

(above) Baby Stephanie in Korea,
before she became a Burke.

(right) Tim and Christine greeting
Stephanie on her arrival in America.

(below) Stephanie and Daddy in 1991.

Stephanie grows
into a charmer.

The photo on the right
was taken in 1992.

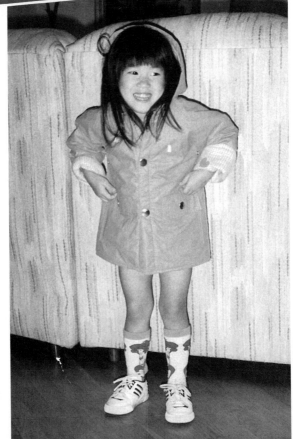

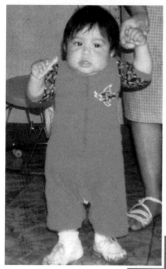

(left) Ryan in Guatemala
before he joined the Burkes.

(below) Tim and Christine
at the orphanage in Guatemala
to pick up Ryan, who is held
by a staff person (back right).

(above) Christine and Ryan
with Joe Padilla, who helped the Burkes
with Ryan's adoption Guatemala.

(right) Stephanie and Ryan share a hug.

(above) Ryan and Stephanie during his first Christmas in America.

(left) Christine and Ryan shortly after he became part of the family in 1989.

(below) A dapper Ryan in 1990.

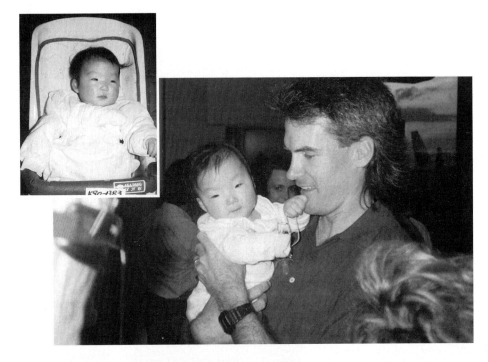

(upper left) Nicole in Korea before her adoption.

(above) Tim holds Nicole at the airport on her arrival in the States.

(above) With her mom helping, Christine gives Nicole a haircut in the hospital.

(right) Christine holds Nicole for the first time following her open-heart surgery in Montreal.

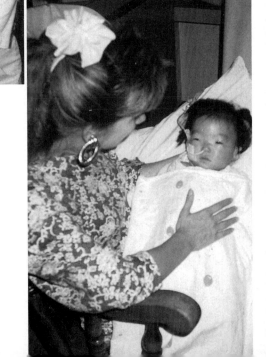

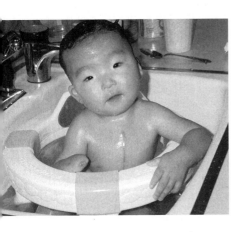

(top) Nicole cheek to cheek
with her favorite guy.

(above) Nicole takes a bath
after her surgery in 1991.

(right) A thankful mom holds
her now-healthy girl.

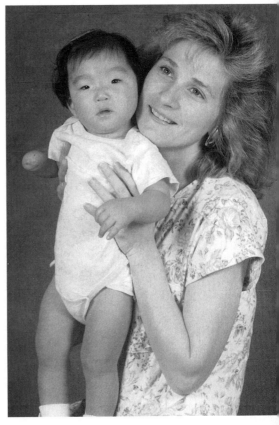

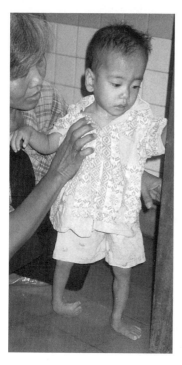

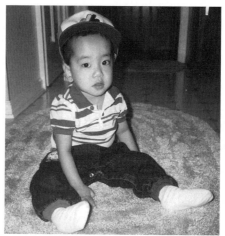

(above) Wayne in Vietnam before becoming a Burke.

(above right) A much healthier-looking Wayne six months after coming to America.

(right) Tim and Wayne at home following Wayne's clubfoot surgery.

(above) Wayne, on the right,
with his new brother.

(left) Mommy and Wayne,
Christmas 1993.

(below) Wayne and
sister Stephanie
in Colorado.

(above) Tim, a Green Bay Packers fanatic, forces the family to dress accordingly in the Burkes' 1992 Christmas picture.

(right) Stephanie and Ryan playing shepherds in 1990.

(below) Daddy and the kids at a playground in 1992.

(above) Wayne and Nicole
playing together.

(right) Ryan not enjoying a hug
from sister Stephanie.

(below) Kisses for Nicole
from Stephanie and Mommy.

(above) A "pile on Daddy" party in 1991.

(right) Stephanie holding her little sister.

(below, left to right) Nicole, Ryan, Wayne, and Stephanie in early 1994.

(top, inset) Tim and Christine's engagement picture.

(above) The Burkes on a weekend getaway in 1991.

(right) The young couple on their wedding day.

(above, left to right) Young Christine, brother Bill, and sister Susie.

(right) Christine's dog Benji, who lifted her spirits following her accident.

(right) Christine and her brother and sister picking up their mom in a limousine on her retirement day.

(lower right) The Burkes with Grandma Holt, the founder of Holt International Children's Services, in1990.

(below) Sister Susie and Stephanie in 1991.

(above) Young Tim,
the future major leaguer.

(right) Tim and his dad
at the ballpark.

(far left) Tim's mom,
who died when
he was 16.

(left) Tim's brother,
Dick, who first
predicted Tim
would become a
major leaguer.

(right) Terri, Tim's sister, with Stephanie in 1987.

(below) Tim's dad and stepmother, Carol,
with Ryan and Stephanie in 1990.

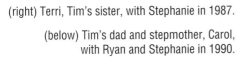

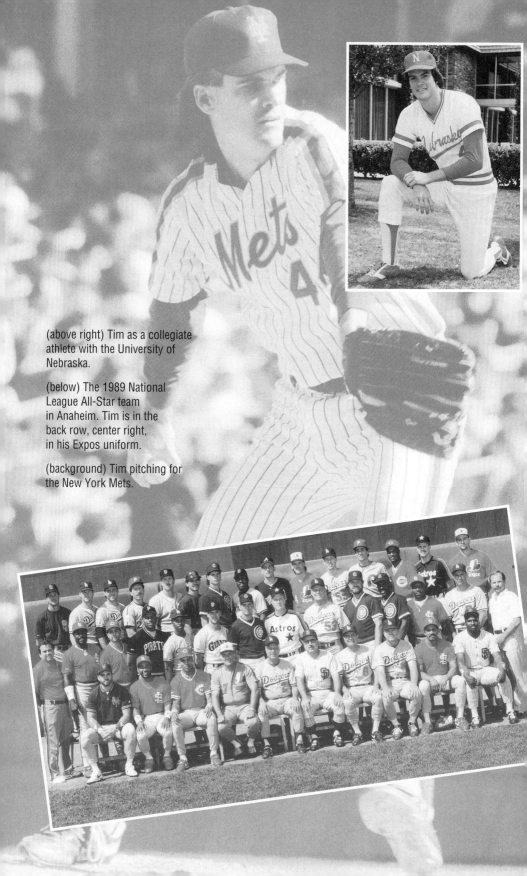

(above right) Tim as a collegiate athlete with the University of Nebraska.

(below) The 1989 National League All-Star team in Anaheim. Tim is in the back row, center right, in his Expos uniform.

(background) Tim pitching for the New York Mets.

CHAPTER TWELVE

Bad News

Christine
♥♥♥♥♥

WHAT WE DIDN'T KNOW THEN WAS THAT WE WOULD SOON NEED that new, stronger foundation for our marriage.

From the time Tim and I had met five years earlier, we had talked about having children. Early in our relationship, I realized Tim hadn't given fatherhood a lot of thought. His biggest dreams for the future all revolved around his baseball career. But as we fell in love and he realized my feelings on the subject, he quickly began sharing my family goals.

Perhaps due in part to my own difficult family background, I always dreamed of the day when I would bear children and have a normal family of my own. After struggling all my life to establish a healthy self-identity, I think I subconsciously viewed motherhood as a fulfilling role that would somehow make me a more complete and valuable person. As far back as I could remember, I longed to be a mommy. And the deeper my love for Tim grew, the more I dreamed about one day being the mother of his children.

Having children would have been difficult the first few years of our marriage. Our transient, empty-pockets life-style was not at all conducive to a "normal" family life. But once Tim made the majors, those factors changed. We were both ready for a baby. Buying our first house, a place of our own where we could begin to raise our family, only heightened our anticipation. I could imagine a nursery and baby toys scattered over the living room floor.

As many couples discover, however, feeling ready for children and actually getting pregnant are two very different things. Month after month in Montreal, and then back home in Omaha, we were disappointed by our failure to conceive. We encouraged ourselves with the experience and wisdom of friends who told us, "It often takes time."

The progression from disappointment to discouragement was tempered somewhat by the anticipation of Tim's second major-league season. The difference in our attitude going into 1986 was almost indescribable.

For the first time in four seasons, Tim was beginning a year with the same organization he was with the season before. And for the first time in his career, we went to Florida in February knowing where we would be going the first of April to live for the summer. While Tim had to work hard to get in shape for the season, the old pressure was gone. The excitement and antici-pation of a new season were still there. So was Tim's competi-tive drive to pitch well and improve on every performance. We could enjoy the spring sunshine, however, without the long weeks of uncertainty we lived through during the past years.

Perhaps the nicest difference of all hit me when we broke camp and headed for Montreal. For the first time in our married life, I made a move knowing what to expect and where we were going. I was no longer a rookie's wife.

Some players don't like playing for one of the Canadian teams. Going back and forth through customs can be a hassle. And a lot of red tape is involved when you earn your livelihood and live half the year outside the United States. In Montreal, there's also a big cultural difference. Downtown where we lived, most of the people spoke French, so everything from reading street signs to grocery shopping presented a challenge. But we accepted it as an adventure. We enjoyed getting to know Montreal and looked forward to another year there.

Fortunately, Tim never experienced baseball's dreaded sopho-more jinx. On May 26, when he pitched in his one hundredth major-league game, he became the quickest pitcher in baseball history (after only 202 games on a big-league roster) to reach the century mark in career appearances. But his ongoing professional success couldn't offset my growing concern about our failure to conceive a baby. Something had to be wrong.

Sometime around midseason, I made my first appointment to see an obstetrician/gynecologist with experience treating infertility. I gave her my medical history, including how long we had been trying to get pregnant. I worried that the physical injuries I suffered in my car accident when I was 14 were part of the problem. But Dr. Sennecca reassured me on that point and set up a series of fertility tests. "We'll want to run some tests on your husband, too," she said. "Will that be okay?"

"I'll talk to him," I told her.

I could imagine how Tim would feel about that prospect. Just the idea of fertility testing seemed a terrible invasion of personal privacy and dignity. So when Tim readily agreed to go in with me for the tests, I knew it was out of love for me. He realized how much it meant to me.

The long wait for results was even worse than the tests themselves. Weeks passed. Then one August afternoon when I was home alone in the apartment, our phone rang.

I answered, and Dr. Sennecca greeted me. "I have just received the lab reports on your tests, Christine," she said. "You might want to sit down before I give you the details."

It's that bad? I wondered. "Okay," I said once I got situated. "What is it?"

"Well," she said, "I'm afraid I don't have very good news about your husband's tests."

At that precise moment, I heard a key turn in the front door lock, and Tim walked in. My heart sank. I wanted to protect him from the news; at least I didn't want him to see my initial reaction. So I interrupted the doctor with, "Just a minute, please." I cupped my hand over the phone and whispered to Tim, "Honey, could you please run back out and buy me some 7UP? I'm suddenly feeling very sick." (That was certainly true.)

"Right now?" he asked.

"I'm sorry, Honey. I know you leave for the ballpark in an hour. But I need it before you go."

A perplexed look crossed his face as he looked at me. I felt so transparent. So awkward. "Would you mind?" I pleaded.

"Okay, sure," he said. "I'll be back soon."

As the door closed behind him, I took my hand off the phone. "I'm sorry," I told the doctor. "I didn't want my husband to hear right now."

"That's all right," she said. "I understand."

She proceeded to read me the test results. "What does that mean?" I asked. She said that while my results were not great, they weren't too bad, either. Tim's, however, were very bad.

I tried to absorb the words. "Then what are you saying?" I asked.

"I'm saying, Christine, that based on the results of these tests, I would have to say that it's extremely unlikely you and your husband will ever be able to conceive a child."

When I hung up moments later, I was in tears. *How can I tell Tim?* I wondered. I didn't want to be as blunt as the doctor; I wanted to soften the blow.

By the time Tim returned a few minutes later, I had regained a little control. "That was the doctor on the phone," I said. "I'm sorry about sending you out like that, but I was afraid for you to be here when I heard the results of our tests."

"What did she say?" he asked.

As I gave him the details, I began to cry. He put his arms around me and held me for a while, saying over and over, "I'm sorry, Christine. I'm really sorry."

I didn't want to go to the ballpark that night. But I didn't want Tim looking up in the stands and worrying when he didn't see me, either. So I went, breaking down and crying again in the wives' lounge, where a number of women hugged me and cried with me.

Tim

THE TEST RESULTS WERE A SHOCK TO ME. BUT I CAN'T SAY THEY devastated me the same way they did Christine. Over the years, as we talked about starting a family, I began to anticipate what it would be like to be a father. But the thought that I might never have children wasn't a terrible personal blow. What I felt the worst about was Christine's reaction. She was obviously hurting. If the test results could be believed, the problem was more mine than hers, which meant I was at least partially responsible for her anguish, whether or not I could help it.

I hated that. But I had no idea what I could do about it.

As I helplessly watched Christine grieve those next few weeks, what I didn't know was that her mind had begun to work on a plan.

One night near the end of the baseball season, Christine made reservations for us at a nice, quaint, little, European-style restaurant in Montreal. The waiter seated us at a cozy table by the window, overlooking busy Saint Catherine Street. We ordered our appetizers and had started to eat when Christine brought up a subject I perhaps should have—but hadn't—seen coming. "You know, Tim," she began, "what really breaks my heart about our test results is the thought that I'll never be anyone's mommy." Her voice cracked with emotion. "I've always wanted to be a mommy."

"I know," I told her as I reached over to hold her hand. "I'm sorry."

"I've been thinking," she continued. "How do you feel about adoption? Would you consider adopting children? Could you find it in your heart to adopt a baby?"

I hesitated to respond. There was no easy answer to her question. I knew what my immediate, gut-level reaction was: *No.* But I also knew how important having a child was to Christine. And if I hadn't understood it before, I thought I did after the past few weeks. It was such an emotional issue for her, I knew I needed to choose my words carefully.

Realizing I had to say something, yet feeling certain I knew how Christine was going to react, I made perhaps the hardest, most painfully honest statement of my life: "I have to tell you, Christine. I just don't think I could love someone else's child enough to be a father. I really don't. I think the idea of adoption is great. I really respect people who do it. I just don't think it's for me."

I could see the anguished look on Christine's face as she said, "Do you realize that would mean we'll never be parents?"

I nodded. "I understand that, Christine. But I just don't think I could adopt. I'm sorry." I didn't know what else to say. I felt horrible—guilty and a little ashamed to be saying it. I especially felt bad for Christine.

Christine
♥♥♥♥♥

I COULD TELL HOW TERRIBLE TIM FELT, SO I DIDN'T PUSH THE ISSUE any more that night. Instead, I changed the subject, and we each made our most valiant effort to enjoy the meal and the remainder of the evening.

I knew that many marriages are destroyed or damaged by the conflict and strain resulting from infertility. I loved Tim too much to want that to happen. So driving home that night, as grieved as I was, I silently prayed, "Lord, I believe You know what's best for us. Maybe You know that having children to carry around would be too hard on my neck and back. I'm going to have to trust You, Lord."

I sensed in my heart that I would never be able to change Tim's mind. I had never before seen him so dead set in his opinion on anything. So a few days later, when Tim was gone on a road trip and I was home alone in our Montreal apartment, I got down on my knees and began to pray, "Lord, I ask that if it is Your will for us to have children, please change Tim's heart. If it's not Your will, then take the desire for children out of my heart. But no matter how it works out, please let our hearts be one, so this doesn't tear our marriage apart."

I can't say God immediately took away the pain I felt, but I did experience a measure of peace that the entire issue was out of my hands and in God's control.

Tim's second successful major-league season came to an end as he finished with a 9-7 record and a solid 2.93 ERA in 68 appearances. However, the Expos missed the playoffs again.

Back in Omaha for the off-season, I began to think about getting a second opinion on our infertility tests. As much as I dreaded the idea of more tests, I just couldn't give up all hope of having children.

One day I worked up the nerve to ask Tim, "Do you think . . . maybe . . . we could try a few more tests?"

I could read Tim's true feelings on his face. But he said, "Okay. I know how much it means to you."

We began another unpleasant round of testing, which for me included monthly ultrasound tests to try to determine the exact time of ovulation and blood tests every other day to chart the pattern of my changing hormones.

Tim
✦✦✦✦

ONE FALL MORNING, I GOT UP EARLY, LEFT CHRISTINE ASLEEP IN BED, and hurried to my doctor's office, where I had been scheduled for a more thorough infertility test.

As I stood in the doctor's office and he began part of my exam, I started to feel a very strange sensation. The next thing I knew, I was slumped back on the examination table while the doctor applied a cool, wet cloth to my forehead.

"What happened?" I asked.

"You passed out," he said.

"What do you mean?"

"You fainted."

I felt terribly woozy at that moment. But my embarrassment was far worse. I had never fainted before in my life. These tests were absolutely humiliating. After I rested a few minutes, the doctor said I should be okay.

Christine was still asleep when I returned home a little later. When I sat on the side of the bed and put my head in my hands, she awoke, rolled over, and asked, "What's wrong, Honey?"

I described what had happened.

"How do you feel now?"

"Mostly I feel humiliated."

"Oh, Tim!" she said as she took my hand in hers. "That's it. I've put you through enough. No more testing. It isn't worth it. I just want you to know that I love you more than any child we could ever have together. We're not going through any more of this!"

Part of me thought, *What an incredible relief!* But I couldn't help feeling guilty about my reaction.

Christine
♥♥♥♥♥

I PROMPTLY CANCELED A SCHEDULED LAPAROSCOPY (A SURGICAL procedure involving an abdominal incision and a visual examination of the uterus), which didn't please my doctor. But after months of testing, I wasn't going to put my husband or our marriage through any more. If further fertility testing was going to be so unpleasant and so stressful, I truly did feel *It's not worth it.* And that honest reaction made me wonder if perhaps God was, indeed, answering my ongoing prayer by changing my heart.

One night not long after that, I had a most remarkable dream. In it I saw Tim in a store, holding a baby girl in his arms. I knew she was a girl because Tim was standing in front of a rack of clothes, buying her a dress. All I could see of the child were her eyes, which were big and round and slanted, so I knew she was Asian. And the other impression that struck me was how much Tim loved that little girl. I don't remember how I could tell he absolutely adored her; I just knew he was nuts about that baby in his arms.

When I awoke the next morning, the dream remained so vivid in my mind that I remember thinking, *Wow! What does that mean? Is God trying to tell me something here?*

In my mind, I could still picture Tim loving the little girl with the almond eyes. "No way, Lord," I prayed. "He won't consider *any adoption*, let alone a foreign baby." But the dream had seemed so powerful, and the feeling I had seeing Tim with that little girl was so encouraging, that I got out of bed and drew a picture of what I had dreamed, just to make sure I remembered.

That night, we went to the home of another couple who hadn't been able to get pregnant. This girlfriend and I had been part of a four-woman support group we called "The Infertile Myrtles." I told her about the dream, but I didn't tell Tim because I didn't want to pressure him. I continued to pray privately, however, that God would change either his heart or mine.

One day in December, we were driving down Dodge Street on the west side of Omahá, and out of the blue Tim said, "I don't understand it, Christine, but ever since I woke up this morning, I've had a deep desire in my heart. I keep thinking we ought to adopt a little Korean girl."

The whole world began to tip and spin. I suddenly felt so dizzy, I didn't know whether I was going to get sick or faint.

CHAPTER THIRTEEN

Stephanie's Story

Tim

I WAS NEARLY AS SURPRISED AS CHRISTINE. MY THINKING HADN'T wavered all fall. Even when some close friends told us they had decided to pursue adoption, I was happy for them and thought their plans were great, but I still didn't think adoption was for me.

Not until I woke up that December morning with a strange new desire for a Korean baby girl did I realize my feelings about adoption were suddenly different. I remember thinking, *It's as if my heart has been changed.* And while I always knew I could change my mind, I also knew only God could change my heart.

Any remaining uncertainty was blown away when Christine recovered enough to speak. She confessed she had been praying behind my back. Then she told me about the dream she had— of me holding and loving a little Asian girl. As she talked, I felt a chill go down my spine. She showed me the sketch she had drawn of the dream, and we just looked at each other in stunned amazement. *God had to be in this.*

We spent the last few weeks of the off-season talking to people and trying to learn what was involved in the adoption process. But what no one we talked to could tell us was how we would even begin to go about adopting a Korean girl.

Early in the 1987 season, I met a guy in New York who happened to know something about foreign adoptions. He gave me the names of a couple of orphanages and said, "I think you need to talk to the folks at an agency called Holt International Children's Services. They're a Christian group specializing in foreign adoptions. The only problem is that you can't adopt through their organization unless you live in one of the states where they have a local office. But at least they could answer some of your questions and tell you how to get started."

When I got home, I told Christine what I had learned about Holt International. "Let's call them," she insisted.

"I've tried to reach their headquarters in Oregon a couple times but haven't gotten through," I told her.

"Let's try again now."

This time we got an answer. I told the woman who answered that we were interested in a foreign adoption and wanted information. She politely informed me that in order to adopt a Korean child, we had to live in a state where Holt had local offices.

"What states does that include?" I asked.

There were only five—but the third one she listed was Nebraska (with the office in Omaha, no less!).

"You have an office in Omaha?" I said. "That's our hometown!" I turned to see Christine about to burst with excitement. Without a doubt we knew, *God is still working here.*

Christine
♥♥♥♥♥

WE IMMEDIATELY CALLED HOLT'S OMAHA OFFICE AND TALKED TO a caseworker there. When she learned we would be in Montreal all summer, she suggested we begin our paperwork for the application process as soon as we returned to Omaha after the season. But we decided not to wait. We filled out some initial forms, then scheduled the required home visit by the agency's social worker for major-league baseball's All-Star break in July, the only time Tim and I could both get back to Omaha before October.

We climbed on a plane minutes after a Sunday afternoon ball game and flew to Omaha for Tim's three-day break. We spent the next day and a half furiously cleaning our townhouse from top to bottom, thinking, *This lady is going to find us unfit to be parents if we don't get rid of every speck of dust in the place.* Poor Tim spent his only vacation of the summer slaving like a chambermaid.

Our little townhouse was polished, shiny, and nearly antiseptically clean when the social worker rang our doorbell. I wanted to impress her with a grand tour of our spotless home. She could have run a white glove over the top of any door frame. I would have been glad for her to open any drawer or peek in any closet of our house.

Instead, however, she asked to go someplace where we could talk comfortably. We ushered her into the living room, where she sat on our freshly vacuumed couch, opened her briefcase, and took out a long questionnaire we had filled out and returned earlier in the application process. After asking us to clarify a few of our answers, she asked how our families had reacted to the idea of our adopting a foreign child.

"Some family members seem very excited about it. But some aren't," I told her honestly. "Is that bad?"

She smiled reassuringly and said, "That's pretty common."

She asked a little more about our family backgrounds, then about how we thought a child would fit into our professional baseball life-style.

Approximately an hour after she arrived, she closed her notebook, assured us everything seemed to be in order, and said it was time for her to leave. As we walked her to the door, it was all I could do not to beg, "*Please* look at our house! You don't know how hard we worked to make it look this good. Don't you need to go to the bathroom or something?" I wanted to challenge her, "Come on, just try to find some dirt, any dirt. We dare you."

But I bit my tongue, letting her leave without so much as sticking her head into another room of our house. And we flew out the next day for Montreal, where we would play out the season and wait—first to hear if we were approved to adopt, and then to hear when we might get a baby.

The first word came quickly; we received approval to adopt! But who? And when? The people at Holt warned us those questions would take a while longer, perhaps as long as six months.

That's when I began to wrestle with a few lingering doubts. What had bothered me after the social worker's home visit was her response to the one big question I had for her: "Since we both feel so strongly about it, what do we need to do to adopt a little girl?"

"Since this is your first child, you don't have that choice," she told us. "Once the Korean government clears your paperwork, you'll be informed when a baby is available. You won't be able to specify a girl or boy."

God's leading had seemed so excitingly clear in our decision. He showed me a baby girl in my dream. And then when He changed Tim's heart, Tim wanted a little Korean girl. So I wondered, *What if the baby Holt has for us is a little boy? Would that be a sign from God that we shouldn't take him? We just want a child; I know we would love a little boy. But we've based everything on the thought that we'll get a little girl. What if we don't? How will I feel?*

For two weeks after the social worker's visit, I prayed about it. Still I did not feel any peace. Then one day in Montreal, I walked into a baby shop and stood in front of a rack of clothes on sale. A precious little, white, satin dress with matching baby booties caught my eye, and I pulled them out to look closer. And as I stood in the store, it was as if the Spirit of God spoke to me and asked, "Christine, do you trust Me enough to buy this dress?"

I thought, *I don't think I do. I just can't be sure we're going to get a little girl.* So I hung the dress back on the rack.

But after I stood there a few more seconds, I pulled the dress back off the rack and said, "I'm going to trust You, Lord." Then I bought the outfit and took it home to tell Tim the story.

Several more weeks passed. While Tim was on a seven-day road trip, I went back to Omaha to take care of some personal business and to get the house ready for our off-season there. One morning as I began to get out of bed, I felt an overpowering need to lie back down and pray.

"Lord," I prayed, "I'm so anxious. I want a baby so badly. But I'm afraid. I want a little girl. I want what You showed us. I want it all to work out the way You showed us. But Lord, I want to trust You with it and put it all in Your hands."

The very moment I said "Amen," the phone rang. I rolled over and reached for the phone.

"Christine," said a voice on the line, "this is Cathy Kroeze at Holt International. I'm calling to tell you we just got a referral." My heart nearly stopped. "Would you and Tim be interested? She's a little girl. She weighed three pounds at birth. She's a month old now, and . . . "

I thought I was going to faint. "I don't believe this," I told

Cathy. "I was . . . just lying here . . . praying . . . then you call . . . a little girl? . . . I can't believe . . . "

As I pulled myself together, I said, "Of course we'll take her. But you'd better let me talk to Tim first. Please hold the baby for us."

Tim
❖❖❖❖❖

THE EXPOS WERE IN PHILADELPHIA WHEN CHRISTINE TRIED TO reach me. I left the team's hotel that morning to spend the day visiting relatives in the area, and it wasn't until I got to Veteran's Stadium in the afternoon that my roommate, Mitch Webster, told me, "I took a call from Christine today. She wanted you to call her as soon as possible. She sounded kind of upset."

I rushed to the clubhouse phone and called our home in Omaha. "Christine, I'm sorry," I told her. "I've been gone all day. Mitch just gave me the message that you called. He thought you sounded upset."

"I'm not upset," she assured me. "We got a phone call today."

"Really? What phone call?"

"Holt has a little girl for us." She began to cry, but finally she was able to add, "I'm supposed to call them back. What should I tell them?"

"You'd better tell them YES!" I said with a laugh. It was all coming true. I was going to be a father.

Christine
♥♥♥♥♥

I PHONED HOLT WITH FINAL CONFIRMATION OF OUR DECISION. I was ecstatic, and I could tell that the ladies in the office were excited for us. They explained it could be another few months, however, before all the details were final and we could get our baby.

"You know," I said, "as soon as the season is over, Tim and I are scheduled to go with some other Christian ballplayers to Korea to conduct baseball clinics and give our testimony in schools and churches there. Do you think we can actually see our little girl while we're over there?"

Cathy seemed doubtful, explaining that Korean government red tape and regulations made it unlikely. "But before you leave," she added, "we'll see what we can work out."

Her uncertainty didn't dampen my spirits at all. As soon as I hung up, I jumped in the car and went out to buy enough cute bunny wallpaper to decorate a nursery.

The remainder of Tim's third big-league season is a vague blur in my memory. All my thoughts focused on plans for our little girl and the upcoming trip overseas.

Now that we had received official word, we began talking about what we would name our daughter. We reviewed family names and pored over baby-name books. Nothing seemed quite right until one night when I drove Tim to the ballpark and we listened to a "Focus on the Family" radio broadcast on the way. Dr. James Dobson played a tape on his show that day—a lady's incredible personal testimony. The woman, Stephanie Fast, explained that she had been abandoned on the streets of Korea as a small child and endured terrible suffering and abuse. At age six, she had been placed in an orphanage for the next three years. When she was nine, an American couple came to the orphanage to meet the children and pick out a child to adopt. When Stephanie was introduced to them, she actually spit on them. Her voice broke as she asked, "Why would a child who needs love so badly turn around and spit on the one person who seemed to love her? Because I was just too afraid to let people love me."

The couple walked out of the orphanage that day, prayed about it overnight, and returned the next morning to say they had decided to adopt Stephanie. She eventually learned to accept not only their love, but also God's love. And she later became a missionary, telling others about the difference that love can make in a person's life.

As I drove to the ballpark, I thought about the tiny baby we were about to adopt. I prayed that she would never resist our love or God's. But if she did, I thought, *What a wonderful story to relate to!* I knew then that I wanted to name our daughter Stephanie.

We still hadn't reached the ballpark when I told Tim. He said,

"You're not going to believe this, but I was thinking the same thing." It was decided.

Tim

BEFORE WE COULD BECOME PARENTS, I HAD A BASEBALL SEASON TO finish. And for the first time in my big-league career, Montreal was in the thick of the pennant race.

What made the team's success even sweeter was that no one had given us much of a chance at the beginning of the year. Andre Dawson was gone, and Jeff Reardon had been traded. Buck Rodgers told us pitchers that we would have a "bullpen by committee." Everyone would have to do a little of everything.

As the season wore on, I found myself pitching the best baseball of my career. From July 1 to the end of the season, I went 7-0, had 11 saves, and posted an 0.54 ERA. Going into the final week of the season, we were neck and neck with the St. Louis Cardinals atop the National League East.

On Wednesday night of that week, we were two games behind and playing a doubleheader in St. Louis. A sweep would put us dead even with three games to go. But we lost the opener by a run. Then Danny Cox pitched a complete game victory for the Cards in the nightcap. We sat silently in our dugout as we watched the Cardinal players race onto the field to celebrate the eastern division championship we had been dreaming about only hours before.

Our season came to a sad and sudden end. It seemed only a small consolation that I had turned in the best season of my professional career, going 7-0 for the season, with 18 saves and an ERA of 1.19 (the lowest for any Expos' pitcher in 14 years).

Christine

ONCE THE BASEBALL SEASON WAS OVER, ALL I COULD DO WAS THINK about our upcoming trip. The day before we flew across the

Pacific, I phoned Holt and learned that although they couldn't be sure, they thought it might work out for us to see our baby while we were in Korea.

As exhausted as we were after our flight, the first thing we did after clearing customs and checking into our tiny hotel room in Seoul was to pick up the phone and call the number Holt had given us. The woman who answered spoke broken English.

I gave my name, told her who I was, and explained that Holt had made arrangements for me to call. I asked if it would be possible to come and see the little girl we were in the process of adopting. "Yes. You come," the lady said. "But you daughter in hospital."

"She's in the hospital? Why? What's wrong?"

She tried to explain, but I couldn't understand her. So I finally gave up and said, "Just tell me, where is she? How do we get there?"

I managed to write down the address. But when she started giving me directions, I knew I was lost. *How are we going to find this place when we can't even read street signs?* I worried.

Fortunately, a cab driver we found in front of the hotel rushed us to the address the woman gave me. It turned out to be Holt International's Korean office. The lady I had talked to on the phone was waiting for us. "Come with me," she said. "I take you see you baby."

She led us out the door, through a couple of dark alleys, and two blocks along another street to a small street-front clinic. As we walked through the door, my heart pounded with the realization, *Our little girl is inside!* Quickly we followed her down a hallway and into a tiny nursery filled with maybe a dozen baby beds. "There you baby," she said, pointing across the room.

As we rushed those last few steps toward our little girl, it seemed the world shifted into superslow motion. My feet wouldn't move fast enough.

A fragile little bundle of life weighing just over four pounds, she was lying in her bed, having just recovered from a case of pneumonia. So beautiful. But so tiny and helpless.

Tim and I both began to cry. And Tim, who had never been comfortable around babies, who I thought was a little afraid of babies and never seemed to like them, immediately reached down into the crib without a moment's hesitation, swooping up Stephanie and holding her ever so gently in his arms.

The two of them bonded in that instant. I kept weeping as I observed an incredible look of love and devotion I had never before seen on my husband's face. I thought, *The dream has come true, Lord. Look how much he loves this little girl!*

I didn't even mind that Tim was hogging her. I just stood crying tears of overwhelming joy as I watched the man I loved more than anyone else in the world snuggle and kiss the tiny little stranger who was soon going to be our daughter. I marveled at what I saw: *How can this be? He didn't beget this child. But he's acting like he did. He's the epitome of the lunatic, first-time father whose wife just gave birth to their baby girl!*

For the next 45 minutes, we held and kissed Stephanie. Tim even let me hold her for a few minutes before we finally had to say our bittersweet good-byes and leave her.

Tim
◆◆◆◆◆

WHEN WE TALKED ABOUT THE POSSIBILITY OF SEEING STEPHANIE in Korea, I wasn't sure I wanted to deal with the pain I knew we would face being with her for such a short time and then having to walk away, knowing it could be several more months before we would see her again. But I was glad we did.

We actually got to see Stephanie a second time the day we flew back to the States. She had recovered enough from her pneumonia to be out of the hospital, so her foster mother brought her to Holt's office to meet us for another 25 minutes of love and affection. Christine and I, along with our friends Tom and Carin Roy, placed our hands on Stephanie and prayed, thanking God for this incredible gift of life and asking the Lord to protect her and bring her safely to the U.S. as quickly as possible.

Almost two months passed before the December day the Holt office called to say, "Your little girl is ready to leave Korea. She'll be arriving in four days at the airport in Des Moines, Iowa."

Christine's sister, Susie, her brother, Bill, and a couple of other friends all squeezed into our car for the drive to Des Moines. We arrived at the airport early enough to meet with a group of five other adoptive families waiting for Korean children on the same flight. One of Holt's staff briefed us on the procedure.

All the regular passengers would deplane first; then the escorts with the babies would come off last; and so on. The meeting ended about 45 minutes before the flight was scheduled to arrive. We all went to the gate to wait.

Christine and our friends were chatting when, about 20 minutes before the flight arrived, I suddenly broke into a feverish sweat. I couldn't talk. I didn't want to talk. So I got up and began pacing the floor. That really didn't help because I was on the verge of a full-blown panic attack. It reminded me of the case of nerves I had before my first major-league game, when I told myself I never wanted to be that nervous again.

But this was worse. Much worse.

I kept thinking, *In 20 minutes, I'm going to be a father, and my life is going to be forever changed. This baby's life will be in my hands. I'll have to provide for her. And I know nothing about caring for babies or being a father. What am I going to do? I've got just 20 minutes to grow up.*

When the plane rolled up to the gate a few minutes later, I was still shaken. Most of the deplaning passengers hung around to watch what was going to happen next. Then the social workers went down the jetway into the cabin to collect the babies and carry them out. The Holt people told each waiting family, "When you see your social worker, you'll know that's your baby."

As the first social worker walked out and handed a baby to the first happy family, I think everyone in the gate area started to cry. Christine wept so hard, she couldn't recognize the second social worker as she emerged holding a baby. "Is that one ours?" she asked. "Is that Stephanie?"

"No," I told her as I leaned and craned to see as far as I could down the jetway. "Here she comes!" I exclaimed before my own eyes blurred with tears. The next thing I knew, I was stretching out my arms to receive our daughter, while family and friends surrounded us with hugs and tears.

The moment I took Stephanie into my arms, I felt a massive tidal wave of love unlike anything I had ever experienced in my life. My panic was instantly swept away. I still didn't know the first thing about being a father. But ready or not, I *was* one. And it was the most amazing feeling in the world.

CHAPTER FOURTEEN

Bad Timing

Christine
♥♥♥♥♥

ON ONE HAND, I FELT AN INCREDIBLE AND UNEXPECTED SENSE OF fulfillment in motherhood. Overflowing with such a pure love for another human being stretched my soul and made me feel more wonderful than anything I had ever imagined. But on the other hand, nothing in my life ever made me feel worse than the soul-shaking recognition of my shortcomings as a mother.

I sought out all the Christian parenting books I could find. But with my difficult family background, reading those books was like trying to understand a foreign language. One day as I was reading Dr. Dobson's *The Strong-Willed Child*, I became so angry that I threw the book across the room. *Who is this guy?* I fumed. *He's nuts! This is impossible.*

Because I had no healthy reference point, it all seemed so unattainable, so frustrating.

I thought it would be so easy and come so naturally. I fully expected to be the calm, consistent, perpetually positive, unconditionally loving, ever-in-control mother I had always dreamed of being. But the first few months of dealing with a colicky child like Stephanie aroused negative emotions that shocked and alarmed me. *If I'm feeling these things dealing with a sweet and helpless baby, how am I ever going to handle a two-year-old's defiance or a teenager's rebellion?*

One day when Tim was gone and Stephanie had been screaming inconsolably for hours, my exhaustion and frustration turned into an all-consuming anger. In fact, I was afraid I would lose control, lash out, and hurt Stephanie. The power of my own emotions scared me so much that I called Focus on the Family to plead for help.

"I'm afraid of myself," I told the counselor who talked with me. "I'm afraid for my daughter. I don't know how not to be angry."

The counselor listened as I described my feelings. Then she asked, "Christine, is there a point at which you consciously realize you've reached the edge and you're about to lose control?"

"Yes, I think so."

"Then when you feel yourself getting to that point, put the baby down in her bed, even if she's crying, and leave the room for a few minutes. Maybe turn on some music and let yourself calm down. Can you do that?"

I told her I thought I could. And as it turned out, I resorted to that strategy numerous times. I remember many days when I would put my crying baby down in her playpen and walk out on our porch, shut the door behind me, and pray as I watched her through the window. Gradually I realized I could control my feelings and not have to worry about hurting my baby.

Fortunately, Tim and I talked about the feelings I was struggling with, and he understood. The day I threw the book across the room, he sat down beside me, put his arm around me, and said, "I realize this is hard for you, Christine. But with God's help, I know you can be the kind of mother you want to be. Maybe you just need to commit to Him your skills as a parent."

Tim was right. When I began to do that, God helped me understand the advice I had been reading, and I started trying to put it into practice. The same books that had frustrated me soon became a comfort and guide, showing me a healthy model that could overcome the patterns of my past.

One of the greatest joys of my life was watching Tim with Stephanie. The dream I had before we adopted her didn't begin to convey the depth of Tim's feelings. Whether he was tossing her in the air and roughhousing the way fathers do or holding her sweetly in his arms and rocking her to sleep, I seldom saw them together without feeling almost overwhelmed by the love in his eyes as he looked at his little girl.

Watching his natural fatherly instincts—his calm, patient gentleness—added a whole new dimension to my love for Tim. To me, he was the model of a godly parent.

Within months, I was so encouraged that Tim and I started

talking about the possibility of another adoption. One day during the '88-'89 off-season, I was leafing through a Holt International magazine when I spotted a picture of a little girl from Costa Rica. The article explained that she had been physically abused and now had serious emotional and physical needs. I was so drawn to the heart-rending picture that I picked up the phone and called Holt's local office to ask if she was still available for adoption.

Our social worker, Cathy Kroeze, pulled the little girl's file and learned that she still didn't have a home. But she quickly discouraged me from pursuing that particular child. "It's a very difficult case," she said, "with a lot of unknowns and potential complications. You wouldn't know what you were getting into, and I would be afraid you just wouldn't be ready to handle her."

I knew Cathy was right. But when I hung up the phone, my heart still ached for that little girl nobody wanted.

Tim knew I made the call. "What did you find out?" he asked. I told him everything Cathy had told me.

Weeks passed. Still I couldn't shake the ache in my heart as I wondered how many other children were out there with special needs.

Finally I said to Tim, "I've been thinking, Honey. Why not adopt a child with special needs? Those kids are a lot harder for the agency to place. I believe we could handle it. What do you think? Would you be willing?"

Tim didn't respond right away, but I could see he was thinking.

"Sounds pretty scary, doesn't it?" I asked.

"Yeah," he admitted. "But let's at least check it out and give it some thought."

I called Holt and set up an appointment for us to go in and look through their "Child Waiting" book—a directory of children ranging from six months to 16 years old who hadn't been placed for adoption because of complicated special needs. So many faces. So many different medical and emotional challenges.

When we adopted Stephanie, all we had to do once we went through the approval process was wait for the agency to inform us that a child had become available. We hadn't even been able to specify, "We'll take a girl."

But now we had an entire book full of photos to choose from.

Boys and girls of many different nationalities. And alongside each photo was a brief summary of the case and a description of the child's special needs. Many had cerebral palsy. Some were paraplegic. There were hydrocephalic children. Even little blind boys and girls. Some had been waiting for years. So many children. So many heartbreaking needs. How could we choose just one? How could anyone choose a son or a daughter from a picture and a paragraph in a book?

Tim

WE RECEIVED PERMISSION TO TAKE THE BOOK HOME OVERNIGHT and spent the entire evening looking through it and talking. We looked at pictures of some of the older children until we realized we both felt strongly about wanting Stephanie to be the oldest. So we turned our attention to the baby section of the book.

We each felt drawn to the first little guy pictured, a Guatemalan boy just over a year old. He was cute. But his stubby arms and legs looked all out of proportion to the rest of his body. His head seemed to sit directly on his torso, with little or no neck. *Is he deformed?* we wondered. The photo almost made him look that way.

We kept looking. But after paging through the book again and again, we kept coming back to him. We were a little uneasy, but we agreed to call the next morning to find out more about him.

Christine phoned Holt. "What can you tell us about him?" she asked.

"Why don't you come in and take a look at his medical report?" Cathy suggested.

His medical file was a half-inch thick. The poor child seemed to have had everything from hypothyroidism to herpes, from pneumonia to parasites.

We asked permission to show the file to a local doctor for his assessment. He called us that evening after looking it over. "If you're asking my advice," he told us, "I would discourage you from adopting this child. With his hypothyroidism undiagnosed and untreated for the first eight months of his life, plus the malnutrition, he could very well be retarded. The other problems I see here can all be treated. But there could be things that haven't shown up yet. There are just so many unknowns."

When we hung up after talking to the doctor, Christine and I were both quiet for a while.

"I feel guilty for feeling scared," I admitted. The little boy obviously needed the kind of love we could give him.

After wrestling with our conflicting feelings for a while, we finally went to seek the advice of our pastor, Elmer Murdoch. We explained that we both really felt we should adopt this boy, yet were scared and felt guilty about our fear.

Pastor Murdoch listened as we talked. Then he gave us some wise counsel. "You know," he said, "God doesn't expect us to have perfect Christian feelings all the time. What God wants is for us to let Him perfect us through the experiences of our lives. Sometimes we have to step out and do what we know is right, letting the peace of God rule in our hearts to overcome the doubts and fears as we go."

He looked from one of us to the other. Then he asked, "Do you feel a peace and an assurance that this adoption is what God wants you to do?"

We both nodded. We had prayed enough about it to feel confident. And we were willing—just scared.

"Then I suspect," he said, "that if you continue to walk in obedience, your other feelings and fears will fall away."

He was absolutely right. No sooner did we call Holt the next morning to say, "We'll take him," than we both felt a flood of joy and peace that washed away all our uncertainty.

Christine
♥♥♥♥♥

SINCE WE HAD ALREADY GONE THROUGH THE ADOPTION PROCESS once with Holt, things went smoothly and quickly on our end in Nebraska. But bureaucratic wheels grind much slower in Latin America.

Throughout the spring, we continued filling out papers and slowly, step by step, compiling the dossier required by the Guatemalan government. We had to provide police clearances, medical reports on our family, and official copies of our birth certificates and our marriage license, all notarized. We had to assemble a file of recommendations and provide various tax forms. The whole package had to be certified here in the States and then again in Guatemala. After that, we had to begin the process for obtaining the proper immigration forms and taking care of other seemingly endless details. I wondered if we would ever untangle all the red tape.

Spring training in South Florida came to an end for 1989, and we headed north for Montreal and the beginning of another baseball season. Still we heard nothing about when we could fly to Guatemala and get our new son.

The time frame was now completely up to the Guatemalan authorities. We couldn't go before they gave permission, and when they did, we would have to fly down and pick up our son on the date they assigned. Once the season began, our big problem was Tim's schedule. From early April through the first of October, major-league baseball teams never get more than one day off at a time. And unlike starters who only pitch once every four or five days in a predictable pattern, Tim's relief duties required him to be ready to play on any given day.

As eager as I was to go down and get the son we had already named Ryan Richard (Ryan is the name of a good friend; Richard is Tim's dad's name), I couldn't imagine making the trip by myself. We both obviously needed to go. *What if we get the call now?* I wondered. *How can Tim go during the season?*

The frustration and worry of waiting was somewhat eased that spring by the exceptional year Tim was having. Since Jeff Reardon had left the Expos after the '86 season, Tim was now the team's primary closer, and he quickly piled up saves early in the '89 season. Pitching in 22 games over one two-month stretch, he went 2-0, with 11 saves and a 0.85 ERA. He was definitely hot.

Then one day in June, we got a call from Cheri at Holt International. "How would you like to go to Guatemala?" she asked.

"You're kidding!" I exclaimed. "When?"

She laughed, enjoying my excitement. "Probably around the middle of next month. We'll let you know as soon as we get exact dates."

It was wonderful news! A short time later, we received even more wonderful news when the Guatemalan authorities said we could arrive to pick up Ryan on Monday, July 10—the first day of the annual three-day All-Star break. It was the only free time Tim would have until the season ended in October. We could go meet Ryan together. It seemed almost unbelievably perfect, an obvious answer to prayer, and a final confirmation from God that we were doing the right thing.

Tim

THE DAYS CREPT BY SLOWLY.

The weekend before the All-Star break, the Expos played a series against the Astros in Houston. I arrived in town early on Thursday, an off day. Christine and Stephanie were flying in later that day to link up with me and Christine's brother, Bill, who was going to take Stephanie to Grandma's house in Omaha when Christine and I left for Guatemala City on Monday morning.

I was in the team's hotel, with an hour or so to kill before Christine arrived, when I decided to get something to eat. Just outside the hotel restaurant, I heard someone calling, "Hey, Tim!" Rich Griffin, the Expos' public relations director, rushed across the lobby wearing a big grin on his face. "I'm glad I caught you," he said. "I've been looking all over for you. I have some great news for you."

"What's up?" I asked.

"We just received word a few minutes ago that Tommy Lasorda [manager of the L.A. Dodgers and NL All-Star manager that year] picked you to be one of the pitchers on the All-Star team. Congratulations!"

"Me? You're kidding!" I said.

Unbelievable, I thought. I felt stunned—proud—thrilled—and a million other emotions all at once. I had been named to the National League All-Star team. Incredible.

Then it hit me. *The trip.*

"But I'm planning to fly to Guatemala Monday," I told Rich.

"I know," he replied.

"I don't know what to say, Rich."

"I hate to rush you, Tim," Rich said, "but you're going to have to make your decision quickly. I've got a press conference set up this afternoon to announce your selection. Again, congratulations!"

I hurried back upstairs to my room, closed the door, and cried, overwhelmed just to have been selected for the All-Star team. It was an honor I had hardly dared dream for and certainly hadn't expected. *Tommy Lasorda actually picked me?*

But wrapped tightly around all the positive emotions was an almost choking sense of frustration over the choice I knew I needed to make. I realized I would have to turn down my first and possibly only chance to ever be a major-league All-Star. In a way, it was a simple decision. As much as the honor meant to me, going with Christine to get Ryan was more important than any baseball game.

Of course, that didn't make the decision any less painful.

CHAPTER FIFTEEN

All-Star Son

Christine
♥♥♥♥♥

WHEN TIM MET US IN THE HOTEL LOBBY, I IMMEDIATELY COMMENTED on his red and puffy eyes. "Allergies?" I asked.

"Hay fever's been bad," he said.

But he sounded awkward trying to brush off my concern. In the excitement of his greeting for me, Stephanie, and my brother, Bill, I let it go. But I sensed something was wrong.

Bill and I wanted to eat, but Tim was strangely insistent on going up to the room first. "We can eat after you get settled," he said. We all went upstairs together. Once we got to his room, Tim said, "I probably ought to tell you the real reason my eyes are red."

"I knew something was up," I told him.

He gave me a sheepish grin. "I've been picked for the All-Star team."

I screamed in excitement, "You're kidding!"

"No," he said. "Can you believe it?"

I hugged him, and Bill shook his hand.

"Oh, Honey! That's wonderf . . . " My heart sank as it hit me. I could see Tim studying my reaction as I asked, "But what about Guatemala?"

"I already decided I'm not playing," he responded.

"Hold on," I said. "We need to think about this."

"There's a press conference at 6 o'clock. That's when I have to announce my decision."

"But this is an opportunity of a lifetime. Maybe you should think . . ."

"I'm going with you to get Ryan," Tim insisted. "That's a lot more important than any baseball game."

"Let's at least pray about it," I said. So Tim, Bill, and I all prayed. Then I asked, "Since we have a little time, would it be okay for me to have a few minutes to myself to pray?" When they agreed, I slipped into Bill's adjoining room, closed the door, sat in a chair, and opened my Bible.

"Thank You, Lord," I began. "But what are You doing? And why now?" I told God He knew I was too scared to travel to another country alone. I needed Tim. But I also recognized what the All-Star selection meant to him.

As I prayed for an answer, a verse suddenly came to mind. I looked it up to be sure: "Peace I leave with you; my peace I give you. I do not give to you as the world gives. Do not let your hearts be troubled and do not be afraid" (John 14:27).

When I rejoined Tim, I told him, "I think you ought to play."

"I can't," he insisted. "I need to be with you."

I told him God had given me a verse.

"What verse?" he asked skeptically.

I told him about my prayer and read the verse. He was unconvinced.

"Honey," I said, "I know you really want to go with me. But maybe you can catch a red-eye right after the ball game. You'll be down there Wednesday morning in plenty of time to come back with us and help us through customs."

"Well . . . let me see," he reluctantly agreed, picking up the telephone. "I'll call and check the flight schedule. But if I can't fly out right after the game, I won't even think about playing."

"Okay," I conceded. Fortunately, the All-Star game that year was in Anaheim. There was no trouble finding a midnight flight from L.A. International Airport to Guatemala City.

"Are you sure?" he asked me.

"I'm very sure," I insisted.

Tim booked the new flight and hurried out to the press conference announcing his selection to the 1989 National League All-Star team. His excitement and happiness seemed so obvious that I refused to think about the international trip I was scheduled to make—*alone* now—the next Monday morning.

Tim

I UNDERSTOOD AND APPRECIATED WHAT IT MEANT FOR CHRISTINE TO insist I play in the All-Star game. Her response epitomized the way she always thought about her family first. I was so thankful for her sacrificial love. Thus, while I trusted her spiritual instincts, I couldn't shake the guilt I felt over my excitement at making the All-Star team. That excitement built as the weekend wore on.

Our Saturday afternoon game with the Astros happened to be NBC's Game of the Week. Prior to the game, NBC caught wind of our Guatemala trip, so I answered their questions about our decision to adopt Ryan and our plans for the coming week. Then during the game, unknown to me, NBC broadcasters Bob Costas and Tony Kubek retold the story to a national television audience.

That resulted in a message that was waiting for me when I walked into the visitors' clubhouse at the Astrodome Sunday morning. A man whose name I didn't recognize had called to say he had seen the game on TV the day before and had heard about our trip to Guatemala. The message said he wanted to help in any way he could. He left a local number to call.

Professional athletes get a lot of strange messages in clubhouses. My policy was to never return a phone call unless I knew something about the caller. But as I reread this particular message, I got an odd sort of feeling about it.

I picked up a phone and called Christine back at the hotel. I told her I had to hurry out to the field for my pregame workout, but I thought maybe she should phone this guy and find out what his message was all about. I read her the note and told her, "I have a feeling. I think this may be from the Lord."

Christine

I NEVER HEARD TIM SAY ANYTHING QUITE LIKE THAT BEFORE, BUT I trusted his instincts. So I decided, *If he thinks I should call, I'll*

call. I dialed the number and said, "Joe Padilla, please."

When he answered, I told him, "This is Christine Burke. My husband, Tim, asked me to call you regarding a message you left for him at the Astrodome today."

"Oh, yes," he replied excitedly. "I was watching the game yesterday and was thrilled to hear of your plans to adopt a little Guatemalan boy. You see, I'm from Guatemala."

He did have an accent.

"I'm also a Christian," he went on. "And when I heard the story, I wanted to help if there was any way God could use me."

I still wasn't sure about this guy. But he continued, "I'm an official with Aviateca, one of the airlines flying into Guatemala City. Perhaps I could help with some of the arrangements for your flight."

"Our adoption agency has already booked our flights," I replied. I pulled out the tickets to take a look. "We're on . . . Aviateca." *Wow! His airline,* I thought.

"Good," he replied. "Our airline will take good care of you. Perhaps I can help make hotel arrangements in Guatemala City. I have a good friend who runs one of the best hotels there, the El Camino Real."

I looked at our reservations. "That's where we're staying!" I said. *So it's a good hotel; that's reassuring.*

"I'll call my friend and make sure you get the very best attention from him and his staff."

When I thanked him for his kindness, Mr. Padilla said he wished he could do more. "I'll call you before your flight tomorrow to make sure everything is on time," he promised.

I tossed and turned all night, too excited to sleep. When my alarm finally went off at 6:00 A.M., I thought, *At least I can quit lying here watching the minutes change.* I was showered, dressed, and already packed before 8 o'clock, when the phone rang. It was Joe Padilla.

"I hope you had a good night's sleep," he said.

"No mother sleeps well when she's in labor," I said with a laugh. "I just want to get this trip over with and bring my son home."

"I'm sure you're feeling anxious about making this trip by

yourself," he said. "My wife and I were praying about this last night. We decided, if it would be all right, that I would be happy to fly to Guatemala with you. I can help you through customs, show you around town, help you get where you need to go. Anything you need."

I was speechless. My mind raced. *Either this is the world's slickest con man, or Joe Padilla is an angel.* Which was it? An absolute stranger was offering to escort me on a trip to a foreign country. He sounded sincere enough, but for all I knew, he could have been a psychopathic killer. Tim had flown out to the west coast after the game the night before. I would have to make this decision on my own.

If this wasn't legitimate, accepting his offer would be a serious mistake. On the other hand, if God really was in this, I shouldn't turn the man down. I remembered what our pastor had said: "Let the peace of Christ rule your hearts."

"Are you sure you want to do this?" I asked.

"It's really no problem."

"Well . . . okay, thank you," I said, praying that this was the right thing to do.

Mr. Padilla told me he would meet me at the airport before my flight. So as I walked into the terminal, I was thinking, *Have I lost my mind? I must be nuts. Lord, please let him look like a respectable businessman and not a psychopath!*

Approaching the Aviateca counter, I noticed a gentleman dressed very professionally in a nice suit and tie. *Lord, please let that be him!* He looked quite sane as he smiled beneath a small, black mustache. "Are you Christine Burke?" he asked.

When I said I was, he shook my hand and introduced himself: "I'm Joe Padilla."

He asked to see my ticket, and when I handed it to him, to my great surprise, he walked around behind the counter and checked me in himself! Based on the way the ticket agents deferred to him, I guessed he must be one of the "head honchos" with the airline.

During our long flight, this charming man told me all about his family and how much he loved them. Then we compared stories of our personal spiritual pilgrimages. He told me all about what God had done in his life.

I had no real clue what this man's presence would mean to me, however, until we actually landed in Guatemala City. It seemed everyone in the airport knew him: "Hello, Mr. Padilla." "Yes, Mr. Padilla." "Hi, Joe!" "Hey, look, it's Joe Padilla." You would have thought the man was royalty. Customs officials greeted him warmly and waved us directly through, not bothering to look in my suitcase or even ask me why I had come to Guatemala.

Joe (by now that's what I was calling him) went to pick up a rental car (he wouldn't let me pay for it) while I waited outside the terminal and met representatives from the orphanage. Two women, Gloria and Blanca, briefed me on the procedures we would follow when I went to the orphanage to meet Ryan the following day. But we cleared customs so quickly that Joe convinced the ladies to let me go to the orphanage that afternoon and at least see Ryan for a few minutes.

I was excited as I rode through the streets of Guatemala City thinking, *I want to soak in every detail. I want to remember everything I see, everything that happens here, so that some day, years from now, I can tell Ryan about the day I met him.*

As we pulled up in front of the orphanage and I saw the tiny building and the yard behind iron bars, I felt an incredible sadness mixed with my anticipation. *This is where my son has lived. He's somewhere right behind those walls.*

Climbing out of the car and walking toward the building, I thought my knees would buckle. My emotions did. Overcome with tears of joy, I worried what Gloria and Blanca were thinking. "Tell them I'm just so happy, Joe," I said. "Tell them I'm not sad. I'm just so happy."

Joe translated, laughing. They all laughed as I cried and kept saying, "I'm so happy. I'm just so happy."

When we got inside, the two women led us down a hall. As we passed each room, I thought, *Is this it? Is he in here?*

Blanca stopped outside the last room. "Tell Señora Burke," she told Joe, "her little boy is here. We'll bring him out to her. But she should step back because he'll probably be afraid." Joe translated.

A minute later, an orphanage worker walked out carrying Ryan. The moment I saw him, I fell in love. *He's the most beautiful little boy in the world. And he's ours!*

But he was afraid. He wouldn't come to me. I took out a sucker I brought for the occasion, but he wouldn't take it from me. Finally I gave it to Blanca, who handed it to him. He stuck it in his mouth, looking at me out of the corner of his eye.

The ladies told us Ryan had been very sick with parasites. His severe case of diarrhea would require medication before he could possibly travel. When Joe heard that, he insisted on calling a pharmacy and going out to get the prescription filled that evening.

While he was gone, I had a few more minutes with Ryan. But every time I tried to hold him, he screamed and pulled away. "It will take time," Gloria assured me. I could understand that much in Spanish.

After we left the orphanage and checked into the hotel, I prayed and thanked God again for sending Joe Padilla. Yet I remained terribly concerned about Ryan's fear. "Lord, I don't want this to be traumatic for him," I prayed. "I know he's scared. Please change his heart so that he will fall in love with me, too."

The next morning, when Joe and I went to the orphanage, the same lady brought Ryan out to us. I held out my arms, and he immediately reached for me. I had him all day. And by the time we finished signing papers at the American embassy, I was getting him to laugh as he played around my chair. He was falling in love with his mommy, and she was certainly in love with him.

After taking him back for his last night at the orphanage, I returned to the hotel Tuesday evening, famished but too exhausted to accept Joe's dinner invitation. I just wasn't up to eating in a restaurant surrounded by strangers. So I went to my room and called room service for an order of black beans and rice. As I polished off my simple supper, I reviewed the incredible experiences of the last few days. Tim's surprise selection to the All-Star team. The decision to come to Guatemala alone. Joe Padilla. The trip. Meeting Ryan for the first time. The bad news about his health. The change in him today.

With my supper almost gone, as an afterthought really, I

clicked on my hotel room television. When the screen came to life, I screamed in amazement to see a broadcast of the All-Star game—live from Anaheim, California!

The inning after I turned the game on, Tim walked out to the pitcher's mound. For the next two innings, I couldn't stop pacing around the room, alternately cheering and talking to the TV, rooting for Tim. After everything that had happened the past few days, after all God had done for me, it was as if He decided to top off everything with this. Sitting in my hotel room in Guatemala City, Guatemala, I was watching my husband pitch in a major-league All-Star game taking place in an entirely different world.

Unbelievable.

Tim

CHRISTINE HAD CALLED THE FIRST NIGHT TO TELL ME ABOUT MEETING Ryan. As much as I wished I was with her, I was having a memorable time of my own amid all the All-Star hoopla. What a thrill just to be part of it!

I was trying to absorb the reality of it all after the team's workout at Anaheim Stadium on Monday afternoon. From a back corner of the clubhouse, I was enjoying my relative anonymity as I watched throngs of reporters crowd around such big-name teammates as Will Clark and Ryne Sandberg. After a while, one reporter sauntered my way. He had heard something about my plans to go to Guatemala and asked me a couple of questions. As I began to fill him in on the story, another reporter drifted over. Then another and another, until I had a huge crowd around me, all furiously taking notes—not about baseball, but about the trip and our plans to adopt Ryan.

On Tuesday, *L.A. Times* writer Bill Plaschke did a nice, long feature about our adoption plans. On the field before the game Tuesday night, ESPN asked for an interview. And just before game time, one of the ESPN producers came up to me and said, "I realize this is kind of last-minute, and that what you're doing is a very personal thing. I'll understand if you feel sensitive and don't want to do this. But if we can make the necessary arrangements to get a film crew on your flight after the game, would you consider letting us go down to Guatemala and do a story about your adoption?"

I didn't know what to say. I didn't know how Christine would react to the idea. It could be a real invasion of our privacy at such a personally significant time. But what really struck me as I considered the request was the thought, *Maybe this could encourage some other people to consider adoption.* I thought of all the pictures I had seen in the "Child Waiting" book, all those other special-needs children who still didn't have a home. "Okay," I told the producer. "If you can arrange it, we'll cooperate for a story."

Then it was game time. When word came down to the bullpen that I should warm up, I developed a major case of butterflies. I got the call to start the bottom of the fourth inning.

As I began my sprint from the left-field bullpen, the thought hit me: *Slow down. Stop and realize where you are. This is the All-Star game.* I slowed to a walk and tried to soak in every sight, sound, and feeling on my way to the mound, past Howard Johnson at third and Ozzie Smith at shortstop.

Bo Jackson led off against me and singled to right for the American League. But I got Wade Boggs to ground out. Kirby Puckett flied to center. And I ended the inning by striking out Harold Baines. I didn't bat in the fifth, so Lasorda left me in for the bottom of the fifth. I got the leadoff hitter when Julio Franco flied to right. But then Cal Ripken sliced a double. Ruben Sierra bounced to first, moving Ripken to third with two outs. Mark McGwire came up and hit a ground ball into the hole at short. But Ozzie Smith knocked it down with a backhand stab, pounced on the ball as it bounced once in the dirt, and rifled a throw to first—beating McGwire by an eyelash to prevent a score. My dream-come-true outing was over. I had faced eight American League All-Stars and hadn't given up a run.

The minute the All-Star game ended, I grabbed my suitcase and a friend drove me to L.A. International. The ESPN film crew was already there waiting for me, tickets in hand.

I called Christine from the airport to say I was on my way and tell her, "Guess what? I got to pitch two innings."

"I know," she said with a laugh. "I was eating black beans and rice and watching you pitch!"

"Uh . . . Honey . . . " I hesitated. "Would it be all right if I brought a camera crew along?"

"A what?"

I told her about ESPN's request.

"Do I have a choice?"

"Well . . . not much," I admitted. "They're already here, and they have tickets."

"Okay," she said. "If you think it will encourage people to adopt, why not?"

My adrenaline high wouldn't let me sleep on the flight. *What a night!* I was thrilled just to be an All-Star. But to pitch well— *incredible! And now I'm on my way to meet my son in the morning!* How could I sleep?

Our flight landed at Guatemala City early Wednesday morning. The ESPN team hit a snag at customs because they had left in such a hurry that they hadn't received the proper clearance or signed the correct permits to carry their expensive equipment into Guatemala. Fortunately, Joe Padilla, who had driven to the airport to pick me up, came to their rescue. When he learned what was going on, he vouched for the camera crew, explaining that they were with him and promising they wouldn't sell any of their equipment illegally during the brief time they were in the country. At that, the customs people shrugged and waved us all through.

I had an exciting reunion with Christine at the hotel, then we went together to the orphanage to take custody of our son.

Christine had told me how frightened of her Ryan had been at first. So as we walked into the orphanage, I nervously wondered, *Will he like me?*

He went straight to Christine, but he wasn't sure about me. The three of us went out into the tiny orphanage yard of dirt and gravel to be alone for a while. Christine had a little bottle of bubbles, so I entertained him with those and tried in vain to get him to warm up.

As excited as I felt walking out of the orphanage with Ryan

that day, I also felt a real burden of sadness. Getting into our car and looking back at the rundown, little building where Ryan had lived for so many months, I thought, *That was his entire world. There are so many other children still there, behind that wall, beyond those iron bars. I wish we could take them all.*

We spent the rest of the day sightseeing and getting a flavor of Guatemala. ESPN shot enough footage for a story that won an Emmy that year for a short sports documentary.

We left for home on schedule Thursday morning with Ryan. Since he still wasn't sure about me, Christine gladly held him on her lap the entire flight.

Sometime during the trip, she noticed my All-Star ring for the first time. In the excitement of the past couple of days, I had forgotten I was wearing it. I took it off and handed it to Christine.

"It's beautiful!" she said.

"Look what's engraved on the side."

She turned the ring and held it up to the light. "July 11, 1989."

"You know," I told her, "that date means a lot more to me than the All-Star game. That's the day you signed the papers at the embassy completing the adoption. So that's the date we officially got our son."

I looked down at the little boy sleeping peacefully in Christine's lap. I thought, *Some day, this ring will be his.*

The Expos were beginning a series with the Reds that night, and we landed in Cincinnati right at game time. I caught a cab to Riverfront Stadium and slipped into the dugout in the middle innings. My surprised teammates greeted me with handshakes and congratulations.

Buck Rodgers sent me to the mound in the ninth. I struck out the final batter and earned my eighteenth save of the year, tying my career high.

What a day! What a week!

CHAPTER SIXTEEN

Nicole's Story

Christine
♥♥♥♥♥

NATURALLY, ONE OF THE FIRST THINGS WE DID WHEN WE GOT HOME with Ryan was to set up an appointment with a pediatrician in Montreal—a tiny lady who conducted a battery of tests in her office. Tim and I stayed with Ryan throughout most of the procedures, comforting him when he cried, easing his fears, and keeping him calm while the doctor took blood samples and gave him a thorough physical examination.

We had been warned about the potential damage caused by Ryan's hypothyroidism, which had gone undiagnosed and untreated for eight months after his birth. We noticed his obvious lethargy, the way his tongue often hung out of his mouth, and his dull, distant stare. But we were hopeful that a better balance of thyroid medication would soon spur his development.

The doctor said the results of the blood tests would determine Ryan's thyroid prescription. *Surely that will increase his alertness and energy level,* I thought.

"Well, doctor . . ." I began after the tests were done, anxious for reassurance concerning my biggest question. "Uh . . . do you think . . . uh . . . what are the chances that . . . he might someday . . . be retarded?"

The diminutive doctor drew herself up to her full height and looked me right in the eye. "Mrs. Burke," she said, "he *is* retarded."

Tim

WE SHOULD HAVE SEEN IT COMING. I GUESS WE WERE JUST HOPING for the best, because that diagnosis shocked us both. We went home from the doctor's office that day and grieved. We had been on such a spiritual high after all our excitement over the way God had enabled us to get Ryan.

Now this.

I think my strongest initial emotion was anger. To think that just because of when and where he was born, Ryan would never realize his full human potential! Just because he hadn't been delivered in the United States, where a routine blood test conducted on newborns would have spotted his thyroid condition before it did serious damage, he would pay the price for the rest of his life. It all seemed so unfair, so wrong.

Yet even in the throes of our initial anger and discouragement, neither of us ever doubted that God wanted us to be Ryan's parents. So we soon went from devastation to determination. We would do everything in our power to give Ryan the fullest life possible.

As it was, I think Stephanie played the biggest role of anyone in the miracle that took place over the next few months. She was as advanced for her age as Ryan was behind, and she became his teacher, his therapist, and his inspiration.

The contrast between our two children was painful to watch at first. Stephanie would run and play and get into everything an active two-year-old can get into. Ryan would sit and stare, seemingly oblivious to the world his sister experienced and explored.

But Stephanie saw Ryan as a potential playmate and partner. She refused to leave him alone. Never discouraged by his look of disinterest, she would show him over and over how to do something, like climbing up the slide backward. "Come on, Ry-Ry," she'd say, pushing and prodding him to move, to try, until he became a studious copycat.

Stephanie would build a tower of blocks in the bathtub. Ryan would watch and then build his own tower. Stephanie would eat with a fork, so Ryan wanted to learn to use a fork. She learned to drink out of a cup; so did he. She learned to put on her own socks and roll down the tops. Soon he was doing that, too. She would talk (she always talked); Ryan would repeat words after her.

Soon Ryan was talking on his own and showing initiative. The glazed look faded from his eyes, and a lively sparkle took its place. The developmental distance between our two children closed quickly as Ryan began to catch up.

We were astounded by what a little love and attention could do.

Christine

TIM FINISHED THE SEASON WITH A 9-3 RECORD, A CAREER-HIGH 28 saves, and a 2.55 ERA in 68 appearances. He couldn't have picked a better year to have an All-Star season, because his Expos contract was up at the end of that 1989 season. We told our agents we liked Montreal and wanted to stay there, so we'd be glad for a two-year deal. Yet nothing really prepared us for that fall, when the Expos offered a three-year, multimillion dollar, guaranteed contract. The day Tim signed that contract, we felt overwhelmed. I don't think either of us could even comprehend that much money.

The first thing thing I thought of was, *Now I can help Mom! My dream can come true! I can help her retire!* After all the years she worked so hard to support our family, it meant the world to me to be able to do that for her.

One of the biggest thrills of my life came the day she quit her job. I flew home to Omaha, where my sister, Susie, my brother, Bill, and I rented a limo. We were parked outside her office when she walked out the door for the last time. Her co-workers watched as she looked at them and asked, "What's this?" That's when the three of us jumped from the limo and greeted her with a bouquet of red roses. Then we took her out to eat to celebrate the occasion. How thrilling it was for us to honor my mom and all her years of hard work!

The money we earned made it possible for us to help other members of our family as well. One of our special joys was being able to give money to families who wanted to adopt but couldn't afford the expensive ($5,000 to $10,000) process. While it may sound generous, we got a lot out of it ourselves. We had so much fun surprising people and experienced such a sense of satisfaction doing it that sometimes we felt almost selfish. It was like getting to play Santa Claus every year.

Tim

THE OTHER THING THAT EXCITED US ABOUT MY NEW CONTRACT WAS its implication for our future, beyond my career in baseball. By 1989, when I turned 30, I began to think seriously about that future. After the team party fiasco my rookie year and the counseling Christine and I went through following that season, I realized how weak I was, how far I had to go as a Christian and as a husband.

During subsequent seasons, I made a determined effort to seek out as much Christian teaching as I could absorb. I would spend hours alone in my room on road trips, studying my Bible and reading Christian books—from classics by men like A.W. Tozer and Oswald Chambers to contemporary writers like Max Lucado and Josh McDowell. I also listened to tapes by powerful teachers like Tony Evans and Jack Hayford.

In the off-season, Christine and I continued our involvement in Pro Athletes Outreach. At the annual PAO conference, we were exposed to some of the best Christian speakers, biblical counseling, and additional marriage, family, and parenting resources.

The more we absorbed from all this exposure, the more other people—particularly ballplayers and their wives—seemed to look to us for help. We began taking more of a leadership role in Bible studies for my teammates and their wives. Christine began a chapel program specifically for Expos' wives. And in the off-season, we found ourselves doing more and more speaking for churches and Christian groups in the area.

All this experience brought me to the point where I thought we should consider doing some kind of Christian ministry when we left baseball. My new contract would make that easier by providing a financial base enabling us to do that without having to worry about our ongoing family needs.

Christine

BACK ON THE HOME FRONT, WE WERE HEARTENED BY RYAN'S SLOW but steady development into an active, talkative, bright-eyed boy.

I remember my satisfied feeling of thankfulness in 1990 when Ryan developed a sore throat and I took him back to the same little female pediatrician who first examined him the summer before.

She obviously remembered me. But when Ryan sat on the examination table, she took one look at him, turned to me, and then looked back at Ryan. "Is this the same little boy?" she asked.

"He sure is," I said with a grin. "Doesn't he look great?"

She studied Ryan's chart again, seeming reluctant to acknowledge his progress. "Well . . . " she finally said, "he still seems very short for his age."

I wanted to say, "Well, so do you, doctor!" But I didn't. Just seeing her unspoken amazement was satisfying and encouraging enough. I knew Ryan was going to be okay.

Having two bright, charming three-year-olds was a lot of work, but it was also a lot of fun. They helped fill our hearts and our home with so much love that Tim and I began talking about adopting a third child.

Early in the fall of 1990, we called Holt International to say we would like to begin the process of adopting another special-needs child. Then Tim and I earnestly prayed that the Lord would show us whom we should adopt.

Within a week, I began to feel God working on my heart, but for several days I put off telling Tim what I was thinking. Finally I worked up my nerve and hesitantly raised the subject: "I don't know how you'll feel about this, Tim," I said, "but in praying about our next child, I've felt the Lord laying it on my heart to consider a child with more serious medical problems. A much tougher case than Ryan. Do you think that's even a possibility?"

I watched closely as I spoke, trying to gauge Tim's reaction for any sign of reluctance or fear. Instead, I saw him grin and begin to shake his head. "I've been thinking the same thing for days," he admitted. "But I didn't want to say anything because I was afraid you would be afraid." Once again, the Lord had confirmed His guidance by making our two hearts one.

The following Monday, I called Cheri at Holt International and told her, "Tim and I have been praying about this, and this time we both feel strongly led to consider adopting a child with more severe special needs. We thought this was the time to call and tell you."

"Oh, brother!" Cheri said.

"What?" I wanted to know.

She sighed. "There's a case we just received . . . "

"What is it?"

"We've just learned about a little Korean baby. She's three months old, but . . . she's just *too* special-needs."

"What's wrong with her?"

"Well . . . " she hesitated. "It's not that you *couldn't* do it; I'm just afraid it may be heartbreaking. And it definitely would be very difficult with your baseball schedule."

"At least tell me about her."

"Okay," Cheri said. "She has four major malfunctions of the heart that will require surgery immediately. But even if those problems are taken care of, she may still die. It's that serious. Plus there are a number of anomalies. Whatever affected her prenatal development at the time her heart was forming also affected her in these other ways. She was born without a right hand, one of her ears is higher than the other, and her eyes are much farther apart than normal."

I didn't care about her eyes or her ears, or even her hand. I wanted to know more about the heart problems. But Cheri didn't have much information.

"At least let me talk to Tim about this," I told her. "We'll see what we can find out about the heart condition. Can you let us think about it?"

"Okay," she agreed.

That night, Tim and I went to our local library and checked out everything we could find on congenital heart problems and her condition, called *tetralogy of Fallot*. For the next few days, we spent all our spare time learning everything we could about the subject.

We knew from our experience with Stephanie and Ryan that Major League Baseball's health insurance policy would cover our children from the moment we adopted them. But we double-checked to see if it would cover the major heart surgery this little girl needed. It would.

The more we read and the more we talked about it, the more convinced Tim became that this little girl was the one God wanted for us. In my heart, I believe I knew it, too, but I wasn't ready to say yes. I was scared to death.

After almost a week, Tim finally said, "We really need to call Cheri tomorrow. Pray about it tonight. We'll see how you feel in the morning. Then we'll make our decision."

With that, we went to bed, and Tim quickly dropped off to sleep. I lay there beside him, unable to slow my mind. I prayed quietly, "You know, Lord, that Tim can handle something like this. But I'm afraid it would just be too hard for someone like me. I know what it's like to spend months in a hospital. I know what pain and suffering are like. It's just so hard for me to say yes to this little girl. I want to with all my heart. But I'm so afraid. I don't think I can stand to watch my child suffer like that. It's like You're asking me to walk through a fire when I already know what it's like to be burned."

I didn't hear an audible voice from God, but He answered me. I knew it. In my mind, I heard Him as clear as day. As I lay there in the dark beside my sleeping husband, God spoke directly to my heart. "Christine," He said, "suffering and struggling will be different now that you know Me."

I thought back again to the months after my automobile accident. Suffering then, without Jesus in my life, had been like a nightmare in hell. No joy. No hope. It was all fear. But in the years since I committed my life to Christ, He had been faithful to ease my fears. He had given me hope and so much joy. It was true. Suffering *should* be different now . . .

But could I make such a momentous decision based on this one promise? "Okay, Lord," I finally said. "I'm going to trust You with this." It felt like the biggest, scariest step of faith I had ever taken.

The next morning, I told Tim I thought we should do it. We called Holt immediately. Then we waited for all the government red tape on both sides of the Pacific.

Knowing a child you're adopting is half a world away and that you won't be able to see her or hold him for who knows how many months is always hard. But the wait in this case created more than the usual impatience. Because of her medical problems, we didn't know if she would even live long enough to reach the U.S. for the surgery she needed. She was cyanotic, which meant her skin tone was continually blue because her damaged heart barely kept her alive. Her prognosis was not good unless she got treatment soon. That's why, by faith, we named her Nicole Victoria, which means *victorious heart.*

The winter of '90-'91 seemed like the longest off-season ever. As much as we enjoyed the holidays with our two three-year-olds, we couldn't help thinking about Nicole. *When will she get here? Will she be okay?*

We sought out the best pediatric heart specialists in South Florida, planning Nicole's operation for as soon as possible after we got her—in time, we hoped, for all of us to move together from Florida back to Montreal at the end of spring training.

(We had sold our townhouse in Omaha and bought an off-season residence near West Palm Beach the year before. Our thinking had been to establish our permanent base near the Expos' spring training location in order to simplify our lives. Instead of three moves a year, from Omaha to Florida to Montreal and back to Omaha, we would be able to stay in our own home from the end of baseball season in October through the winter and spring training, until the regular season began again in April. Having three hometowns, three churches, three sets of friends, three doctors, and so on had become quite a strain. So our move to Florida had been a real blessing.)

But the timing just didn't work out. Winter ended. Spring training came and went. Still no word. The season began, and we moved back to Montreal for the summer without Nicole. Finally, in late May 1991, we got the call: "She's coming to the U.S. next week."

The Expos would be playing a weekend series in Chicago against the Cubs, so we made arrangements for Nicole to be flown into O'Hare International Airport. As soon as Tim's afternoon game ended, he caught a ride from Wrigley Field to the airport, and we waited with friends for our daughter's flight.

For me, Nicole's arrival was the most emotional of any we had experienced. I remember sitting on the back of one of the chairs in the gate area, watching the plane roll slowly up to the jetway. I leaned against Tim to cry with happiness and relief, thinking, *She's finally here. She's alive. She made it. Now she'll get a chance to live.*

The first thing I noticed as the escort carried Nicole off the plane was her little sleeve rolled back where her right hand would have been. I cried for her loss as I stroked her tiny arm.

What seemed far more disturbing, however, was her coloring. We had seen pictures and thought we knew what to expect. But seeing her tiny blueberry lips overwhelmed us with the seriousness of her heart condition.

While we and our friends were overjoyed at her arrival, Nicole didn't cry at all. She seemed surprisingly content for an eight-month-old baby in an unfamiliar situation, being hugged and held by excited strangers.

Tim hogged her, of course, as the two of them instantly bonded in a way that no longer surprised me.

Tim

WE WENT FROM THE AIRPORT BACK TO THE TEAM'S HOTEL AND SPENT most of the evening in our room entertaining Expos players and their wives. They all wanted to meet our new daughter. It was a memorable night of happiness and celebration among good friends. There was just something about Nicole that attracted people and touched their hearts.

I couldn't look at her without feeling overwhelmed with compassion. Her physical problems were obvious. But it was more the alertness in her eyes, her sweet, gentle nature, and her ready, responsive smile that captured my heart during the first hours we had her.

Yet mixed with our joy was a measure of fear and uncertainty. Doctors warned us that until her heart could be repaired, we should not let her cry. That kind of exertion could cause her to faint or even trigger a fatal heart attack. I remember lying in bed that night, listening to the sounds of Nicole sleeping in her nearby crib and thinking, *How do we keep an eight-month-old baby from crying? Now that she's finally here, will we be able to keep her alive long enough for the doctors to operate and give her a fighting chance?*

Christine
♥♥♥♥♥

SIX LONG, AGONIZING WEEKS PASSED BEFORE WE COULD SCHEDULE Nicole's surgery. Our doctors wanted time to observe, test, and examine her.

In the meantime, everyone in the family fell head-over-heels in love with Nicole. She remained just as amazingly sweet and easygoing as she seemed the first day we saw her. Stephanie and Ryan were crazy about her, wanting to touch her, rock her, and feed her a bottle every time I turned around.

Their three-year-old prayers for their baby sister nearly broke my heart. "Dear Lord," they innocently prayed, "please don't take Nicole to heaven. Help her heart get better so she can stay here with us."

We finally scheduled Nicole's surgery for July 16, the second day of a 13-game Expos home stand. Not only would Tim be with me for the surgery, but he would also be there to help out for the next two weeks.

The morning of July 15, we took Nicole to the hospital and checked her in for all her preoperative tests. Even as we walked through the halls to the pediatrics wing, I felt an overpowering sense of dread I had learned to associate with hospitals. While Nicole seemed oblivious to my emotions, I could tell Tim also felt anxious.

A cheery nurse welcomed us to the pediatrics ward and tried to put us at ease as she showed us Nicole's room and the family area where we would wait during her surgery the next day. But it didn't help us much.

We were still on our little tour when we were paged to the nurses' station. One of the women there said, "You have a phone call, Mr. Burke."

Tim and I looked at each other in surprise. The only person

who knew we were there was my sister, Susie, who was taking care of Stephanie and Ryan. *What could be so important that someone had to talk to Tim here?* I wondered.

"Where can I take the call?" Tim asked.

The nurse directed him to a phone at the end of the hall. I stood holding Nicole and watched him closely as he walked down the corridor. His back was to me, but I saw him lift the receiver to his ear. A few seconds later, I saw his shoulders sag, and I knew what it was.

"I don't believe it," I said softly. "We've been traded."

The nurse gave me a puzzled look. "What do you mean, 'traded'?"

"My husband's a baseball player for the Montreal Expos," I explained. "I think he's just been traded to another team." I didn't tell her he would have to report to his new team immediately. In fact, I couldn't bear to think about all it really meant.

Tomorrow Nicole was going to have open-heart surgery. The doctors told us they weren't sure what they would find; they might not even be able to repair the damage. I was having a hard enough time dealing with the cold truth that this precious little girl I had already come to love with all my heart could possibly die. How could I think about a trade?

CHAPTER SEVENTEEN

Intensive Care

Tim

I HUNG UP THE PHONE AND WALKED SLOWLY BACK DOWN THE HALL, wondering how I could possibly tell Christine. I knew neither one of us could be much more stressed than we already were about Nicole's surgery.

"Christine . . . "

As my own mind groped for the words, she supplied them for me: "We've been traded, haven't we?"

I sighed and nodded. "Yeah," I said.

When Christine closed her eyes, I could tell she was fighting back her emotions. "I don't understand. How could we be traded? How could the Expos trade us now? Where are we going?"

"The New York Mets."

"What do you have to do now?"

"I'll have to call the Mets and tell them I'm not coming right away. I'll tell them Nicole is having open-heart surgery tomorrow and she could die. There's no way I can report until I know she's going to be okay."

But I also knew I couldn't call right away because I wasn't even supposed to know about the trade yet. The phone call had been from Tom Runnels, who had taken over as the Expos' manager when Buck Rodgers was fired a couple of weeks earlier. Tom told me he had learned from General Manager Dave Dombrowski that I had been traded to New York for Ron Darling and a minor-league player. He also warned me that the official announcement wasn't going to be made until 6 o'clock that evening, and he had been instructed not to say anything until it was official. Tom knew about Nicole's surgery and felt so bad, however, that he wanted to give us as much warning as possible. Tom's consideration for us got him in hot water with team management, but I will be forever grateful for his concern and kindness.

When Dave Dombrowski finally reached me at the hospital an hour or so later with official word of the trade, he wasn't happy that I already knew. He gave me a number so I could call and check in with the Mets. Their general manager was very understanding, telling me, "Do what you need to do. Just keep us posted."

We begged the nursing staff to break hospital procedure and let us take Nicole with us for the rest of the day. We couldn't leave her alone, and we both wanted to be there when I broke the news to Stephanie and Ryan.

A very special friend, Wayne Watson, who flew in from Houston to be with us for the surgery, went with me to the stadium. There I went through the painful process of cleaning out my locker and saying emotional good-byes to all my friends and teammates. Next was a very tough press conference.

I think the very first question I was asked was, "How do you feel?"

"How do you think I feel?" I replied. "I'm leaving the only major-league team I've ever played for. I'm leaving my friends. My daughter is having open-heart surgery tomorrow. And in a couple days, I'm going to have to leave behind my wife, my sick daughter, and my two three-year-old children and go to New York."

After the press conference, I went home to face the roughest task of the day, telling Stephanie and Ryan, "Daddy's been traded. I'm going to have to go away pretty soon. But when Nicole gets out of the hospital, you and Mommy will move to a new city to be with me again." They cried.

Much too soon, it was time to take Nicole back to the hospital for the night. I insisted on staying with her for the midnight shift, giving Christine a chance to go home for some rest. Wayne sat with me. Christine returned to relieve us around 3:00 A.M., and I drove home praying I would be emotionally exhausted enough by the day's events to actually get a little sleep.

Christine

SOME WEEKS EARLIER, A FRIEND HAD GIVEN ME A BIBLE VERSE I copied and fastened around the neck of a little teddy bear I now laid gently next to Nicole. The verse said, "Fear not. . . . When you pass through the waters, I will be with you; and when you pass through the rivers, they will not sweep over you. When you walk through the fire, you will not be burned; the flames will not set you ablaze. For I am the LORD, your God" (Isaiah 43:1-3). I clung to that verse, knowing that whatever happened in the morning, I would be able to deal with it.

I thought I would be too keyed up to sleep and too tired to read my Bible or even pray coherently. So I'd brought my Walkman, and I popped in a tape of Scripture and lay down on a cot beside Nicole's bed.

A nurse awakened me before dawn to tell me, "We need to get Nicole up now. It's time for her bath."

I sat upright and looked at my sleeping daughter. "I'd like to do it," I said.

I lifted Nicole carefully from her bed as I whispered softly in her ear, wondering if this would be the last morning I would ever awaken her. After the nurse brought a basin of warm water, I gently sponged her tiny body clean, realizing, *This could be the last time I bathe her.* She smiled when I wrapped her snugly in a big, bulky towel and held her tightly to my chest. Together we savored every precious moment of that morning's routine. I told her, "I love you, Nicole. Thank you for letting me be your mommy."

At 7 o'clock, Tim rejoined me at the hospital to carry Nicole up to pre-op. We waited there a while longer, holding our tiny baby, kissing her, praying, and crying for her. Then a green-clad nurse came into the room and reached out her arms. "It's time for me to take Nicole," she said. And we let her go.

The doctors warned us that even if everything went well, the operation would be long and complicated. First they planned to close up two holes in Nicole's heart; then they would begin a multistep process to redirect the flow of blood in and out of her heart. The doctors' biggest concern was one abnormally small artery leading out of the heart. They were worried that after they made various repairs to the heart muscle, a suddenly normal blood flow might be more than the small artery could take. That problem could, in turn, trigger a heart attack. They wouldn't know until they opened up Nicole whether or not they could make all the repairs at once. They might have to stop the operation, put in a shunt, close Nicole back up, and wait for her to get strong enough for a second operation.

Because we were horrified at the prospect of a second surgery, we focused most of our prayers on the problem artery, praying it would be bigger and stronger than the doctors believed.

Six long, grueling hours passed before a doctor informed us, "We were able to make a full repair." A closer examination of the small artery showed it was a little larger than they had thought. The head surgeon decided chances were better that the artery would handle an increased blood flow than that Nicole would survive a second surgery. "So far, so good," he said. "But the next 48 hours will be critical."

The hardest part of the entire day came next, when Tim and I walked into the intensive care unit. I could barely see Nicole through the tangle of tubes and wires running into and out of her tiny body. I wept as the horrible trauma of it all became agonizingly real for me in that moment.

As I looked down at Nicole, I noticed that for the first time, her fingers and toes, her lips, and her little tongue were no longer blue. Instead they were a healthy-looking shade of pink. Despite all the tubes, despite the incessant beeping of the monitors reminding us how tenuously Nicole clung to life, she looked so much better already. That gave me hope.

I don't know how we would have survived those first days without the support of our family and friends. My mom and sister were there to help with Stephanie and Ryan. Tim's friend Wayne Watson gave him a lot of support. Then there were all of Tim's Expos teammates (or *former* teammates!) and their wives. So many of them crowded the halls outside the ICU, in fact, that we got in trouble with the hospital's nursing staff. "You can't have all those people in here," they told us.

"But you don't understand," I replied. "They're like our family. They care about us."

The doctors operated on Tuesday, and by Thursday, Nicole still wasn't stable. But she was—according to the hospital medical staff—"holding her own." It might be some time before her condition changed.

I encouraged Tim to go ahead and fly to New York, thinking, *He has to leave sometime. If something happens, he can hop a plane and be back in Montreal in an hour. There's no sense both of us sitting here, feeling helpless and unable to do anything.*

When Tim reluctantly agreed, my sister took over my watch at the hospital as I drove him to the airport. "You'll call me if anything changes?" Tim asked. I assured him I would.

We didn't say much else during that drive. I think we were both too tired to do anything but try to hold our emotions in check. Neither of us wanted to voice our worries or even acknowledge our regrets about a separation over which we had no control. We could only hope, and we both did, that the next time we saw each other, I would be holding Nicole in my arms.

I realized Tim was fighting back tears when he put on his sunglasses before we went into the airport terminal. "You need those sunglasses today, huh?" I asked.

He nodded and swallowed hard. He was still wearing them when he boarded his plane after we said our painful good-byes at the gate.

By the time Tim was airborne, I was in the car again, headed back to the hospital and feeling very alone. "Okay, Lord," I said out loud, "it's just You and me now."

Tim

AS MY PLANE PULLED AWAY FROM THE TERMINAL, I FELT AS THOUGH my heart were being ripped out of my chest. I had convinced myself, but only with Christine's help, that I really ought to go to New York, that there was nothing I could do in Montreal. But I could hardly bear to leave Nicole now. I wanted to be there for

Christine. I knew what a drain the long hours at the hospital would be. Then there were Stephanie and Ryan, who would have neither their daddy's presence nor their mommy's attention to meet their needs and ease their worries over the next few days. I felt almost as if I were orphaning my children again by leaving them.

As we lifted off into the sky and I looked down at Montreal, I felt I was leaving behind my entire life. For seven years, Montreal had been my second home. My career had begun there. It was the organization I had worked and sweated for. My baseball friends were all there. Now all those roots and relationships were being ripped away from me.

I left my sunglasses on for the entire flight.

Christine

NO SOONER DID I GET BACK TO THE HOSPITAL THAN I GOT THE FIRST bad word. "We think maybe Nicole had a little seizure," I was told.

"What does that mean?" I asked.

"We don't really know," they said. "We're watching the monitors very closely to see if we can tell anything."

I went out to the waiting room and tried to read for a while. Finally I walked back into the ICU to find a crowd of doctors and nurses surrounding Nicole.

"That's my baby," I said. "What's going on?"

One of the doctors turned toward me. It was the surgeon who had operated on Nicole. Quietly and calmly, he said, "Christine, there seems to be a problem. We're afraid part of Nicole's heart isn't functioning properly. And if it doesn't begin responding soon, we're going to have to operate again."

I took a deep breath. "What would that mean?"

"Well . . . it would not be good."

"So you're saying this is very serious?"

"Yes," he replied. "Extremely serious. At the very best, another surgery will keep her in the hospital for weeks."

"When will you know?"

"I think we're going to have to make a decision in the next half hour." With that, he turned back to Nicole.

I fled the room and took refuge in a small privacy room the hospital kept for families of ICU patients. I closed the door behind me and sank to my knees. "It really is just You and me, Lord," I said. "And if You don't give me the courage and strength, I promise You I won't make it through this. I'll crumble and fall right here."

I had prayed the same desperate prayer a few nights before Nicole's surgery. I felt so afraid. I didn't want to let Nicole go. But as I prayed then, a picture had come to my mind—a picture of Nicole smiling at me as she was held in someone's arms. Because I couldn't see who was holding her, I asked God, "Is that You, Lord? Are You taking her home?" But I hadn't received an answer.

Now, praying fervently on my knees in that little room, the same picture came back to me. The person holding Nicole materialized, and this time I could see she was in the arms of an angel. In my heart, it was as if God were saying to me, "I'm not going to take her now. My angel is just going to be with her and take care of her."

At that I said, "Who am I, God, that You would reveal this to me?" It seemed so incredible. "I never had a father, let alone a Father like You." I felt overwhelmed—and suddenly transformed.

I stood up, left the little room, and headed back into intensive care with an almost overpowering sense of God's presence and peace. Even if they told me they had to operate again, I knew I would be okay. *And so will Nicole.*

Looking steadily into the doctor's eyes, I asked, "Are you going to have to operate?"

"Well, Christine . . . " The surgeon rubbed his hand slowly over his chin. "The area of the heart we're worried about affects the kidneys first. The trouble is she's not urinating. And that's what's worrying us now."

I could hear the uncertainty in his voice. I could see it on his face and in his eyes. He didn't know.

"Oh, Lord," I prayed. "He's just a human being. He doesn't

know what to do. Give him wisdom. Show him exactly what needs to be done for Nicole."

As I prayed, the doctor and I both turned to look at Nicole. He said, "If her kidneys worked, we'd know."

At that precise moment, a blast of urine came shooting through the catheter tube running out from under Nicole's blanket and down into the bottle beneath her bed. I thought, *Hallelujah!* I laughed and said, "How's that?"

He smiled and sighed. "I think that's a good sign."

They didn't have to operate again. Nicole, however, remained in critical condition. She was one of four small children in her ICU section, all hovering between life and death.

The next morning, I was with her when I saw the doctors remove all the tubes from a little boy who had drowned. When they pulled a curtain around his bed and I heard sobbing in the hall, I knew the child had died.

A few minutes later, as I left Nicole's room, I reached the hallway and realized the grieving family was still there. I didn't want to interfere with their grief, but they had seen me, so I couldn't turn back.

As I walked past the sobbing, red-faced mother, she reached out and grabbed my hand. "How's your daughter?" she asked.

"Still holding her own," I responded.

She squeezed my hand. "My little boy just died."

"I'm sorry," I told her. "I don't even know what to say."

She nodded in acknowledgment. "It's so heartbreaking!" She looked around at her family. "But Jesus is already using it to His glory."

I reached out to take her other hand. "You're a Christian then?"

"Oh, yes!" she said.

As I hugged the grieving mother and walked away from her family, I knew in my heart, *The same God supplying her needs right now will help me face whatever is to come for Nicole.* That woman will probably never know how much she encouraged me.

There wasn't a lot of encouragement to be found during the next few days, except for Expos' wives who brought fruit, meals, and emotional support.

Meanwhile, Tim left on an extended West Coast road trip with the Mets. For two and a half weeks, I waited alone, longing each day to have someone upgrade Nicole's condition to "stable." But no one did. Compounding my worry, the other two children in her section of intensive care died. The first was a little girl who had undergone surgery similar to Nicole's.

I was there in the room, kissing Nicole and rubbing her hair as I sang to her, when the monitor across the room went off with a terrible, steady whine. Doctors and nurses ran to the bed from every direction, yanking the curtain closed as they fervently worked to revive the little girl. For 45 minutes, they worked on her heart. Then everything stopped, and the doctor, his head hung down, walked out to tell the family.

I didn't know how much longer I could stand such emotional trauma. One day I asked a nurse to pull the curtain closed between Nicole and the baby girl in the next bed. "I'm sorry," I apologized. "I just can't take any more pain." The next day, she, too, died.

Finally the day came to move Nicole out of intensive care. Tim celebrated the occasion with me over the phone. But my good cheer was short-lived when I realized Nicole wasn't responding normally. She wouldn't smile or reach for me. She spent most of her waking moments staring blankly into space. And she had lost her sucking reflex.

"Something is wrong with my little girl," I told the doctors. "Can it be the drugs she's on?"

They didn't think so, and they agreed to run some tests.

Tim finally made it home to Montreal for one day, the only day I saw him for the first month after he joined the Mets. Fortunately, that was the day we got back the initial test results.

My sister and mom had stayed with Nicole overnight so I could be home with Tim and the other children. Tim and I went to the hospital the next morning. I could tell Tim was alarmed when he saw Nicole for the first time in two weeks.

"She doesn't eat cereal anymore?" he asked.

"No, Honey."

"She doesn't even seem to recognize her bottle," he said.

Tim was trying to adjust to the new reality when a neurologist walked into the room. "I'm afraid I have some bad news," he said. "Nicole's MRI [magnetic resonance imaging test] is not normal. We can't possibly know the extent any time soon, but there's definitely been some damage to the brain."

At least Tim was there to hold me, and I could hold and comfort him. I remember leaving Nicole's room that day and looking back at her through the little observation glass, realizing she hadn't reached for us, protested, or even acknowledged our leaving. The thought hit me, *I don't think she even knows me anymore!*

I stood there, watching her tiny chest rise and fall with each breath, thinking, *Oh, Nicole! We fixed your heart. But what did we do to your brain?*

When Nicole's condition continued unchanged for a few more days, I went to the doctor and begged, "Please let me take her home. She's not getting any better here."

"At least we have a therapist here who can work with her three times a day," he said. "I think that's good for her."

"Well, I have two full-time physical therapists at home. They're three years old, and they'll be terrific for her. They want their sister and their mommy home. And they may be just the stimulation Nicole needs."

"But Christine," the doctor said, "Nicole isn't sucking. She can't take a bottle, and you don't know how to feed her through a tube."

"I can learn," I insisted. "Teach me."

The doctor reluctantly agreed. The nurses showed me how to gently insert a tube through Nicole's nose and down into her stomach. Then we checked out of the hospital. My sister and her fiancé picked us up, loaded our two three-year-olds alongside my very sick baby in the car, and headed for New York to join Tim. As we drove, I hooked a bag of formula above Nicole's head with a hanger and fed her through a tube.

That seemingly insane trip to New York was an all-around success. In the first days we were there, I found a house we could rent for the remainder of the season. And Tim solved the feeding problems with Nicole.

"I know it sounds cruel, but she's got to learn to eat," he said. "Let's not feed her all day. She's not going to starve. But if she gets hungry enough, maybe her instincts will take over and by tonight she'll remember how to suck."

That was a horrible day. Nicole cried pitifully for hours. But when I fixed her a bottle that night and pressed the nipple to her lips, she latched on and gulped down the formula as if she'd never get enough.

"I don't believe it!" I exclaimed to Stephanie and Ryan. "Daddy missed his calling. He should have been a doctor!"

We found great encouragement in Nicole's little accomplishment. And over the next few months, we learned to find what hope we could in the smallest encouraging signs.

CHAPTER EIGHTEEN

Waiting for a Miracle

Tim

PERHAPS OUR BIGGEST ENCOURAGEMENT WAS THE MEMORY OF Ryan's remarkable progress. He had been so lethargic and developmentally backward, but his gradual transformation into an articulate and active four-year-old had defied the doctors' early prognosis and amazed us all.

With Ryan as our only reference point, I think we fully expected the same kind of miracle for Nicole. It was just a matter of time. Whenever she did something new, whether it was turning her head toward a voice or merely smiling, we took notice and imagined, *Maybe this is the beginning.* With her primary heart problems repaired, Nicole did gain size and strength. Her noticeable physical growth encouraged us.

Yet there was no parallel pattern of mental progress for Nicole, as much as we looked for it. It was a hard truth Christine and I couldn't acknowledge to each other because we wouldn't admit it to ourselves. Perhaps our persistent attitude of denying Nicole's real condition delayed our recognition of the first symptoms of an additional problem.

I think it was during the 1992 Mets' spring training in Florida when I first noticed it. I was cuddling Nicole in my arms and talking to her when her chin dropped to her chest for a second or two; then she moved and lifted her head again. When the same thing happened a day or so later, I mentioned it to Christine. She had noticed, too.

It seemed like such a little thing at first. But over the next few weeks, it happened more and more often, and it seemed more noticeable. If I was holding Nicole, it felt as though her entire body stiffened and then went completely limp for an instant before she jerked back upright. Something was definitely wrong.

We made an appointment with a neurologist in New York City as soon as the season opened. We both went in with Nicole for the tests, but before the doctor got back with the results, I had to leave for Shea Stadium.

When I hurried home from the ballpark after the game, I found my sister-in-law, Susie, with the kids. "Where's Christine?" I asked. I knew from the way she said, "In the bedroom," that the test results had not been good.

Christine

THE NEUROLOGIST QUICKLY DIAGNOSED NICOLE'S LITTLE SLUMPING episodes. He said they were a type of epileptic seizure, probably caused by the brain damage Nicole suffered during or after her heart surgery. He ordered an EEG, and I waited in his office for the results.

I saw concern register on his face as he looked over the report. My heart pounded. "This doesn't look good," he murmured, as much to himself as to me. "Not good at all."

Now my heart plummeted. "What are you saying?"

"There's been some pretty serious brain damage."

"How serious?"

He fidgeted in his chair. "It's pretty bad."

I turned and looked at Nicole, sitting in her stroller. "Look at her," I said. "She's sitting up, sucking on a bottle. What do you mean 'pretty bad'? How bad is it going to be? What can we expect?"

He hesitated again. "We'll try to control her seizures with medication. There's no way to know for sure at this point. Every case is different. We'll have to see how your daughter responds."

As devastated as I was by the EEG report, I think we clung to the hope I saw in the doctor's uncertainty: *He couldn't be sure . . . Every case is different . . . We'll have to see how she responds . . .*

We weren't prepared for Nicole to get worse. But she did. Even with medication, her seizures became more frequent and more severe. Her arms would stiffen suddenly and send her bottle flying. If she was sitting up, she'd slam over onto the bed or the floor. If she happened to be standing (she had begun to pull herself upright and stand holding the railing of her bed or the edge of her playpen), her arms would flail out, her chin would jerk down to her chest, her body would stiffen, and she would completely black out and crash unconscious to the floor. We got her a little protective helmet, but that didn't keep her head from banging down or prevent the bloody noses and other bumps and bruises she often sustained when she fell. She always came to after a few seconds, usually whimpering pitifully and looking confused, as if it say, "What happened?"

The seizures increased to 30, sometimes 40 a day. We never knew when another would come. Each one ripped my heart, draining me emotionally as much as they drained Nicole physically.

"She can't take that many seizures a day," the doctor told us. "If you see 40 seizures a day, she's probably actually having 60 or 70. We need to hospitalize her and try to get them under control with medication."

That's what we were doing in the hospital again one morning when I walked into Nicole's room and found a doctor/therapist carefully watching her, just as one of the seizures hit. "Have you seen one before?" I asked the doctor.

She nodded. "I've been watching her for a few minutes. We're hoping the medication will help control those a little better."

"I just wish someone could tell me how serious they are, and how much damage there is to her brain," I said. Our own doctor just wouldn't say.

She got a strange look on her face.

"You know something?" I asked.

"Haven't they told you?"

"Well, they said it was bad," I told her. "But no one has told me whether she's going to be mentally retarded, if she'll get better, or anything."

Now the doctor looked very concerned. "We're just hoping Nicole will be potty-trained one day," she said. "Maybe she'll even learn to dress herself."

I had been thinking in terms like, *How will her seizures affect her dating? Will she ever be able to get married?*

"You're talking about substantial retardation?" I asked.

When she nodded sadly, I put my head in my hands and broke down. She came and sat beside me, putting her arm around me and patting my knee.

In some ways, denying Nicole's condition had been easier than admitting reality. But now every seizure became a sorrowful reminder of the painful truth.

Some days I felt too exhausted to go on, especially with Nicole in the hospital and Tim gone on the road for a week or ten days at a time. I was so discouraged and alone. I don't know what I'd have done without my sister, Susie, who came to help care for the other children.

Early one evening, as I prepared to leave for another long night at the hospital with Nicole, Susie stopped me in the kitchen to hand me a cup of coffee. She said, "You look like you're dying inside."

Exhausted and frustrated, I told her, "I just can't deal with one more bit of bad news!" My body began to shake, and I had pains in my chest. I thought, *I wonder if this is what it feels like to have a nervous breakdown.* I knew I was on the verge.

"I'll stay with Nicole tonight," Susie insisted. "You stay home and try to rest. Spend some time with Stephanie and Ryan. I'll call you if there's something you need to know."

I accepted her offer, grateful Susie was there with me. After she left for the hospital, I thought, *If only my husband understood me as well as my sister.*

The truth was that I was feeling more and more alone, even when Tim was home. I saw how much he loved Nicole, so I knew he had to be hurting, too. I sensed so much sadness in him that I didn't want to burden him any more with my pain.

Tim

I SAW CHRISTINE'S EXHAUSTION. I EVEN IMAGINED HER PAIN. BUT I felt just as frustrated and unable to help my wife as I was to heal our daughter. There was nothing I could think to do. I felt trapped by our circumstances, overwhelmed by my family's needs, and utterly helpless to do anything about them.

Even Stephanie and Ryan began to show the effects of our family's trauma. We noticed it first with Stephanie, who is usually open and transparent about her feelings. One day at the end of a Mets home stand, we all went shopping together at a local mall. Stephanie seemed unusually quiet and distant; she didn't even want to hold my hand.

"What's wrong with Stephanie?" I whispered to Christine.

"She's acting like she's angry with you," she whispered back.

"Why? What about?"

Christine shrugged. "Why don't you try to talk to her?"

So Christine went off with Ryan, while Stephanie and I headed for Baskin-Robbins to get an ice cream cone. Even then she didn't seem her usual bubbly self.

"Is something bothering you, Honey?" I asked. "You don't seem very cheerful today."

At first she denied it. But when I pressed a little, her natural honesty broke through. She admitted she was unhappy. As I probed to find out why, she said she was upset because "you go away all the time to play baseball."

I tried to explain that baseball was how I made my living and that I never liked leaving my family because I loved them all so much. She seemed a lot happier for the rest of the day. But it hurt to realize my four-year-old daughter needed more from me than I was able to give.

Ryan was always a master at hiding his emotions, but his feelings came out in his behavior. When I was gone on road trips, he practically turned into a different boy. He disobeyed, acted up, and threw tantrums. One day in the midst of correcting him, Christine said, "Ryan, what's really wrong? Do you miss Daddy?"

He began to cry. "I don't want Daddy to go away," he told her.

Sometimes when I called home from the road and talked to the kids, they would say, "Daddy, I want you to come home *now!*" Of course, I would feel very bad.

I knew Christine had more than she could do to take care

of Nicole. She couldn't provide all the needs of our older children because she couldn't be mother and father both.

So we talked about the toll my baseball career was taking on our family life. "I don't know if it's worth it anymore," I told Christine. "I used to love everything about the game. I even enjoyed the travel. But I feel so bad every time I have to leave you and the kids now."

It didn't help matters that I had been struggling on the mound all spring. I never got into a rhythm, never found that familiar groove while I was in Florida. Then my pitching problems continued into the regular season. My control wasn't there. And when I did get the ball over the plate, my location wasn't consistent. One day I had decent stuff, then the next day there would be no movement on the ball at all.

The poorer I pitched, the less the Mets used me.

One afternoon during batting practice in San Francisco, sitting in the bullpen at Candlestick Park, my bullpen coach, Dave LaRoche, said to me, "Tim, I know you're going through a tough time with your family. And I suspect you're feeling the strain . . ." Before I could try to deny it, he continued, "I don't want to add any pressure. But I also don't want to see you get hit with any big surprises. So I thought you should know there's been some talk about maybe sending you down to triple-A to get some innings in and let you work out of this slump. We know you can pitch. We still believe you can make a big contribution to the team this year."

Triple-A? I didn't think there was any way my family could deal with another move right now.

I knew Dave as a caring Christian friend. "I feel bad telling you this," he admitted, "because I don't know what's wrong or how to help you fix it. And while I don't think anyone is ready to give up on you yet, I wanted you to know that unless things begin to turn around pretty soon, something is going to happen. You could even get released."

Released? While on one hand I was surprised, I also knew I hadn't been pitching well at all. *Has it really come to this?* I wondered.

That night at the hotel, I told a couple of my Christian teammates, D.J. Dozier and Junior Noboa, what Dave had said. They spent some time praying with me and encouraging me.

Then I called home to break the news to Christine.

Christine

I KNEW IT WAS TIM WHEN THE PHONE RANG SO LATE. "HI, HONEY. How are you doing?" he asked.

"I'm fine," I told him.

"How are the kids?"

"They're all asleep. We had a good day. How was yours?"

"I found out I might be released."

"Tha . . . *what?*"

He briefly told me about his conversation with Dave LaRoche. *Released?* I confess my initial reaction was to think, *Yea! Let's leave New York and go home.* But I also realized what it would mean for Tim. I found it hard to imagine life without baseball. *And I certainly don't want his career to end like this,* I thought.

"I'm sorry," I told Tim. "How are you feeling?"

"I'm okay," he replied, going on to tell me about the guys praying for him. "Maybe it would be for the best."

Tim's reaction surprised me. He had always been such a battler, never a quitter. He always welcomed a challenge. But I knew he had been discouraged when we discussed the added strain baseball was placing on our family. And he was frustrated not to be contributing to his team.

I always had a knack for cheering Tim up when he got down—but not this time. He seemed too discouraged for too long. Or maybe I just didn't have enough left in me to recharge him. Whatever the case, I couldn't seem to bolster his spirits.

I wasn't able to help him with his pitching, either. Tim and I had always joked about it, but throughout his professional career, I had been able to spot the problem when he wasn't pitching well. I watched him so often and so closely that I could usually detect the smallest change in his mechanics. "There's something funny and different about your leg when you come out of your windup." Or, "You're slowing up just before you let go of the ball." Anytime I would tell him something like that, invariably the pitching coach would pull Tim aside the next day and say, "I was looking at the film. You've got your foot pointed just a little bit the wrong way, and you're not being as aggressive as usual. You're slowing down your delivery at the last minute."

But this time, I felt so helpless. The problem wasn't anything mechanical. It was his heart. He didn't want to pitch; he wanted to be with his family.

I wanted to respect Tim's feelings on this. *Maybe getting released would be for the best*, I concluded.

Tim

WHEN I RETURNED FROM OUR WEST COAST ROAD TRIP, I WENT IN to talk to the Mets' new general manager, Al Harazin, face to face. I told him I had heard there was some discussion about sending me down to triple-A. "Even though I have enough years of service to refuse reassignment and force you to trade or release me," I said, "I want you to know that you're my employer and I'll go down if you send me. I feel I owe you that. But I also want you to know that I don't think that will help me. I believe I can work through this just as well right here."

Al told me he had never had a player come and talk to him like that, and that he wished more would. He said he would certainly try to take my feelings into account, but he didn't know yet what the club would decide.

Christine and I talked about what we should do if the Mets made a move, and about whether it was time for me to retire and leave the game. The conclusion I came to was, "I don't feel it's time yet. My three-year contract is up at the end of the season. I'll be eligible for free agency. So I think we should wait and see what happens."

A week and a half later, the Mets made their decision. Instead of releasing me or reassigning me, they chose option number three. They traded me to the Yankees for pitcher Lee Guetterman.

At least we didn't have to uproot the family and move to a new city. We stayed in the same house, and I drove across town to Yankee Stadium. But the trade was another reminder of how quickly things can change in baseball and how little control I had over my own career.

My season took a small turn for the better after I went to the Yankees, but I still didn't get to pitch as often as I wanted. Even so, by the end of the season, I'd lowered my ERA to a respectable 3.20.

What bothered me most about my pitching was my lack of consistency and the effect that had on my confidence. For the first time since joining the Expos as a rookie in 1985, I found myself doubting my ability. *I'm 33 years old. I've been in professional baseball for 12 years now. Maybe I've lost what it takes. Maybe it is time to retire.*

The last few road trips of the season, I invited my brother-in-law to come along and bring Ryan, who needed the extra attention from his daddy. It made a definite improvement in his behavior at home.

But as we approached the end of another season, I still didn't know how to help Christine. Every week, I saw her become more discouraged. Every week, I felt more and more like a failure as a husband.

Christine
♥♥♥♥♥

THE FEW TIMES I BECAME DESPERATE ENOUGH TO ADMIT MY DIS-couragement over Nicole, Tim didn't know how to respond. He either withdrew or told me, "It's going to be okay. We just need to be strong." So I quit talking about it at all. But the only way I could possibly suppress my feelings was to try to deny them altogether. And I paid a lonely price for that.

Two incidents finally penetrated my isolation. The first occurred in September, when I took Nicole to see another neurologist in hopes of finding some new medication to better control her seizures. I dreaded the thought of walking into another doctor's office. But I went out of sheer desperation; Nicole needed some relief, as did I.

I was already tiptoeing on the edge of an emotional abyss when I walked into a huge waiting room crowded with parents and children. I sought out a seat in the far corner, hoping I wouldn't have to speak to anyone. But a little later, a woman with a girl about Nicole's age came and sat in the one empty chair next to me. I didn't speak, but I saw out of the corner of my eye that she was watching Nicole.

At that moment, Nicole's arms jerked out, and her head dropped forward. I knew the woman saw it, but neither of us said a word. A few minutes later, Nicole had another seizure.

This time, to my horror, the woman turned toward me and asked, "Your little girl has seizures?"

Oh, great! I thought. *Now I'm going to have explain everything!*

"Yes, she does," I replied. "We're here to try to get some new medication to help control them." That was all I planned to say.

"My daughter has been having some seizures, too," she said. "We're here to see if we can find out what causes them and what we can do to stop . . ."

A nurse called, "Nicole Burke."

"That's us," I said. "I have to be going. Uh, I hope things go okay for you." Feeling glad to escape, I followed the nurse into the quiet privacy of an examination room. But I wasn't at all glad to hear what the doctor had to say when she joined us.

This neurologist's prognosis was as blunt as the last one's had been hesitant and vague. She came across more abrupt than businesslike. "The MRI shows extensive brain damage," she began. "Besides being mentally retarded, your little girl has second stage epilepsy. That's the hardest kind to control. Many times we can't control it at all."

I was still reeling from this pronouncement when Nicole stiffened in her stroller and sent her bottle flying across the floor. The doctor watched Nicole's seizure, then shook her head. I don't remember precisely what she said, but she wondered why we had adopted a baby "like that."

I became so angry, I wanted to pop her in the nose. I can't recall my exact reply—something meek and unoffensive like,

"Because we love her." But I do remember thinking, *If you have a problem with that, take it up with God, lady!* I was so mad.

The moment the doctor disappeared out the door, I told Nicole, "We're not going to do this anymore! We're through with neurologists. They can't do anything. No more!"

When I finally composed myself enough to leave, I made my way back to the reception area. The nurse behind the desk wanted to know when to schedule Nicole's next MRI. When I told her I wasn't going to have another MRI because there was nothing else the doctor could do, she wasn't happy. So I simply wrote a check to cover my bill and quickly turned to leave.

As I reached past Nicole's stroller to push open the exit door, I glanced back at the reception desk and saw the woman who had talked to me in the waiting room more than an hour earlier. We made eye contact, so I smiled and gave a little good-bye wave.

She held up her hand, clearly signaling a request for me to wait a moment. Reluctantly, I did.

We walked out of the doctor's office together. "How did it go for you?" she asked.

"Not good," I answered, unwilling to explain. "How about you?"

"Not good." She began to cry. "They said my little girl is going to be retarded."

"They did?" I reached out and stopped her stroller. "They said that about my daughter, too."

"I feel so sad," she said. "I'm so worried about her future. The Lord's just going to have to help us."

"You're a Christian?"

When she nodded, I said, "So am I. Isn't that amazing? God knew we each needed another hurting mommy to talk to."

"Are you in a hurry?" she asked. "Could we maybe have lunch and talk some more? There's a cafeteria here at the hospital."

"I would love some company," I told her.

We got some food and pulled our little girls' strollers right up next to each other beside our table. She told me her name was Dolores, and we talked about the kinds of things mothers think about and wish for their daughters.

"Ever imagine her first date?"

"Oh, sure. Even her wedding."

"You, too?"

"I used to try to picture what she'd look like at her high-school graduation. Now I wonder if I'll ever hear her say, 'I love you, Mommy.' "

For the better part of an hour, we traded mothers' heartaches. From time to time, we would drop all thoughts of impossible dreams to watch and smile at our two children goo-gooing at each other.

"Look!" I said with a laugh at one point when Nicole was saying "Da-DA, Da-DA, Da-DA" (her only word) over and over as Dolores's daughter tried to give away her bottle. "Even little retarded girls can try to communicate!"

It wasn't until later, as I was driving home, that I realized that was the first time I had ever acknowledged to anyone that Nicole was retarded. I felt a wonderful sense of release and thought, *Suffering really has been different. In spite of everything I've been through these past few months, God has not abandoned me. He's provided everything I needed to survive. The waters haven't drowned me. The fires haven't burned me. I don't even smell like smoke!*

The second helpful incident took place a few weeks later. When we came home for the off-season, I enrolled Nicole in a small local therapy-and-play group for mentally disabled children. The therapist there told me about a padded crib designed especially for children with seizures. She also suggested that before we invested in such an expensive piece of specialized furniture, I should talk to a local family who had one.

When I visited the family, the mother graciously welcomed me and escorted me upstairs. As she showed me the special features of the bed, she told me about her six-year-old daughter who was playing nearby on the floor. She had suffered a bacterial infection in her blood, which in turn shot her fever so high it had permanently damaged her brain.

"Last year about this time, I was looking through a catalogue with her," this woman said. "She spotted a Barbie outfit and exclaimed, 'Oh, Mom, if I could get that for Christmas, it would be just perfect!' She was so full of excitement and joy about life."

Her voice broke. "This year, I'm not sure she even knows who I am."

Just as she said that, something tugged at my foot. I looked down to see the little girl gnawing on my shoe. I cringed to feel her tongue pressing against my foot.

The mother reached down quickly and pulled her daughter away. I could tell she was embarrassed as she began to apologize.

"You don't need to explain a thing," I said with a smile. "My daughter chews on people, too. Maybe we should get them together some day and let them chew on things together."

The two of us laughed to keep from crying.

Together we acknowledged the difficult circumstances we shared. And I went home encouraged to realize that admitting the truth helped someone else feel a little better.

If only Tim and I could have faced the truth together.

CHAPTER NINETEEN

Searching
for Help

Christine
♥♥♥♥♥

I ENROLLED NICOLE IN A PLAY GROUP FOR MENTALLY DISABLED CHIL-
dren—some were born retarded, and some were affected by accident, disease, or other tragedy. The director was so patient,
answering any and all questions I had for her that first day.

I remember asking, "Do children like this always make it hard
on a marriage?"

The look on her face answered my question even before she
nodded. "I'm afraid the divorce statistics are staggering," she said.

"How do people handle it? What do they do?"

"Some get counseling," she said. "Others can barely talk
about it."

That's us! I thought. Her words pierced my heart. *Tim and I
can barely talk about Nicole.*

I went home that afternoon depressed and asking myself,
How are we going to get through this?

Over the next few days, I felt a tap, tap, tapping on the window of my heart. It was God, trying to get my attention to tell
me He had an answer—prayer.

I didn't want to hear that. *Not again.*

As a Christian, I'd never felt regular, disciplined prayer was a
personal strong point. I hated to admit it, but my most well-
intentioned attempts at prayer often put me to sleep. I'd lie in bed
at night after Tim fell asleep and try to pray. But I'd find myself
nodding off in the middle of a sentence. Then I'd wake up in the
morning feeling so guilty.

When I decided my nighttime prayer wasn't working, I switched
to mornings. But that wasn't any better. I'd be awake, but my mind
would already be on my plans for the day. I'd just get started

praying when my thoughts would interupt: *Oops, gotta call her* or *Need to remember to pick up the dry cleaning.* And if it wasn't my own thoughts interrupting me, it was a child.

I tried everything. *Maybe what I need is one of those fancy prayer notebooks,* I decided at one point. *The one with the flowers.* But no matter what technique, what method I tried, I'd always failed.

This time, however, for some reason, the idea *6 o'clock in the morning* stuck in my mind. My initial reaction was, *You've gotta be kidding, Lord. I'm not a morning person.* Then I thought, *But that's early enough that I can get up and kneel beside my bed long enough to ask God to help Tim and me be able to talk and become close again. Then I can get back in bed and sleep for another hour before I have to get up.*

So that's what I began to do. I'd set my alarm every night and climb into bed. A couple of times the first week, I felt so tired by the time I went to bed that I almost didn't pull out the little pin on my alarm clock. But then I'd tell myself, *It's now or never for our marriage.*

Little did I know how soon my prayers would be answered.

Tim

AT THE END OF THE 1992 SEASON, WE LEFT NEW YORK AND RELO-cated to our new home in northern Indiana. Some friends had told us about the place, and we'd bought it earlier in the year and had been remodeling through most of the season. The house was plenty big for our growing family.

After more than 40 moves in a little more than ten years of marriage, we were ready to put down roots. So we had every reason to be excited about the future. Yet I remained a troubled man.

I was troubled about my baseball career. I'd decided to test the waters of free agency after the season to find out what teams might be interested in me. Since I'd signed my three-year contract with Montreal before I'd been eligible for free agency, this was to be my first chance ever to have a say in where I played. But I found I now had mixed feelings about even signing a free-agent contract to play another year. I'd struggled so during the '92 season, though more with the Mets early in the year, that I still wondered if maybe it was time to retire. Maybe I just didn't have what it took to be an effective major-league pitcher anymore. Pitching certainly didn't seem as fun or as important as it used to.

Along with my baseball future, I was troubled about my family. Nicole's situation, from the hospital stays to the constant seizures, created a steady strain on all of us. My career made that even worse by disrupting our family in many ways. From the beginning of April until October, I was gone from home half the time, unable to be a father to my children or a husband to my wife. Moving three times a year got harder and harder for the children as they grew older, and it greatly complicated medical care for Nicole. I knew I wasn't being the father I wanted to be for my kids or the source of support and help Christine needed.

In the first weeks after the season ended, a good Christian friend helped me resolve the uncertainty I felt about continuing my baseball career with this challenge: "When it's time for you to get out of baseball, Tim," he said, "don't do it because you're afraid you can't cut it anymore. Do it because you're sure it's the right thing to do."

I knew he was right. If I quit just because I had one rough year and was afraid I'd lost it, I might live the rest of my life looking back and wondering, *What if . . .* So I began working out again, deciding to follow through with free agency and determining to go to spring training the next February in better shape than ever.

Christine and I decided to tell my agent I'd entertain offers from any of the five teams (Detroit, Cleveland, Cincinnati, and the two Chicago clubs) within a four-hour drive of our new home. That would enable Christine and the kids to go home to Indiana whenever I went on road trips, providing a measure of stability and continuity for the kids they'd never had before.

Cleveland and Cincinnati made similar offers. Since I felt more comfortable in the National League and I'd always enjoyed playing in Riverfront Stadium, we decided on Cincinnati.

Even after that career decision was made, however, I remained troubled.

The losses I experienced growing up had taught me to try never to show my deepest feelings. As a professional athlete, I'd become a master of self-control. Even my role as a Christian leader and example among my peers seemed a good reason to always try to "be strong." I was now an expert at burying my negative emotions.

But the difference between all the raw feelings I harbored inside and the controlled emotional front I tried to portray—before others, Christine, and even to myself—was so great that the daily effort sometimes drained me to the point of exhaustion. Some days, I didn't even want to get out of bed. I'd rather sleep than have to go on pretending.

Christine
♥♥♥♥♥

THANKSGIVING DAY PROVED TO BE A REAL TURNING POINT FOR TIM. We always looked forward to his sister's visit each year. That day, Terri and I began preparing for our annual turkey feast. Tim remained upstairs in bed, depressed. He didn't want his sister to know.

"Where's Tim?" she asked.

I hesitated, then said, "Well, he's still upstairs in bed."

"Still in bed? It's after noon."

"Well," I stammered, "he's been tired a lot lately."

"Tired? Why?"

"To be honest, I think he's tired because he's really depressed."

Terri just kept peeling potatoes.

"Did you hear me?" I asked.

"Well, yeah. Depressed about Nicole?"

"Yeah, I think so. He doesn't want you to know."

"He needs help. He needs to be strong, I mean, for you and the kids."

I whispered, "No, Ter, I think he just needs the freedom to fall apart."

She thought for a moment, then said, "Oh, Christine, you're right. I don't want him to feel like he's got to pretend around me."

"How about you and I going up there and you letting him know that?" I asked.

"I think that's a great idea!" she replied. "Let's go!"

So up we marched to our bedroom, where Tim was lying practically all covered up. Terri said, "Tim, Christine has told me how you're really hurting. She said you didn't want me to know, but she told me anyway, and I'm glad she did."

Tim looked over at me and rolled his eyes. I shrugged my shoulders.

With a smile, Terri continued: "If you want to stay in bed all day and be depressed, feel free to do that. If you don't feel like saying one word all day long, you go right ahead! That's okay."

Tim smiled and said, "Thanks, you guys."

That Thanksgiving seemed to make Tim aware of how really depressed he was. He came to me shortly thereafter and told me he needed someone to talk to, and he asked if I'd go with him to see a Christian counselor.

Elated, I said, "You bet I will, Honey!"

We got the name of a great counselor in our area, Dan Heiser, and we signed up to begin weekly two-hour sessions with him.

Though we'd been through counseling together seven years earlier, I think both Tim and I felt nervous and uncertain before our first appointment with Dan. But he proved to be such a gentle and caring listener that we found it easier than we'd expected to spend those first couple of sessions summarizing what had been going on in our family over the last few years. What also surprised us was Dan's early observation that our biggest problem wasn't Nicole.

Tim

AT SOME POINT EARLY IN OUR TIMES TOGETHER, DAN COMMENTED that I didn't seem very animated when I talked about my feelings. "It's like you're dead," he said. "There's no passion behind what you're saying." Then he asked what made me get animated.

"I'm animated when I pitch," I replied. "When I strike a guy out, I sometimes react with such intensity of emotion that I almost embarrass myself out there." But I admitted that was the only place I ever really let go and expressed myself like that.

"You need to bring that kind of honest emotional expression and passion to Christine and to your marriage," Dan challenged me.

Then we missed a week of counseling when we went out of town to see my beloved Green Bay Packers. The next time we saw Dan, he asked how the trip had been. We told him, "Not that great." We'd had a fight. Nothing big or drastic by most people's standards. I don't even recall all the details. But we'd come home put out with each other. We'd established a truce, but we never really resolved whatever the fight was about.

Dan asked us to tell him about the fight. We did, trying to recall what each of us had said.

Finally he turned to me and said, "That's an awful way to talk to your wife."

My chin almost hit the floor. His response so surprised me that I sat there with my mouth open, unable to respond.

He hurried on to say, "I realize it's not as if you grabbed Christine by the hair and flung her across the room. I know you'd never do that. Your harsh words seem like nothing compared to that sort of physical abuse. So if you were to compare yourself as a husband to a guy who beats and terrorizes his wife, you'd come out looking pretty good. If he's a one on a scale of one to ten, then you're easily an eight or a nine and feeling good about the kind of husband you are.

"But Tim, that's not the standard God goes by. He's not comparing you to some vicious wife-abuser. In fact, He's not even comparing you to any of the other men you know. His standard is what the Scripture says about cherishing your wife and loving her the way Jesus loved the church."

Christine

THE LONG DRIVE HOME FROM DAN'S OFFICE WAS QUIET THAT DAY. I sensed Tim's growing anger and frustration long before he finally asked sharply, "Do I really speak harshly to you? Am I as bad a husband as Dan said?"

"I don't think he said you're a bad husband," I answered. "He just said you spoke harshly and sometimes weren't tender toward me."

Tim kept his eyes on the road as he asked, "So then, what kind of a husband would you say that I am?"

"Oh, Honey, I don't know."

"No, really," he pressed. "On a scale of one to ten, how am I?"

How do I answer that? I wondered. *As a faithful, loving, supportive husband, I could tell him he's a ten. But as far as being tender, intimate, or passionate, he's more like a three. But I can't tell him that.*

"Christine, just tell me," he said. "Be honest. That's why we're going to counseling. If you want to help our marriage, you've got to be honest." He looked over at me. "So tell me, on a scale of one to ten, how do I rate as our relationship stands right now?"

"Well . . . uh . . ." I stammered. "Honey . . . it . . . uh . . . feels like a three."

The moment I saw the awful look in his eyes, I wished I hadn't answered. But it was too late.

Tim

I FELT ABSOLUTELY DEVASTATED. SO THAT'S WHAT WE TALKED ABOUT in our next few sessions with Dan. And I walked out of Dan's office after every appointment feeling hopeless and depressed. *How could things have gotten this bad without me ever realizing it?* I asked myself.

Because of the spiritual leadership roles Christine and I had assumed over the years among our peers, and because some of the younger players and their wives especially had sought us out for advice, I think we'd come to feel satisfied that our marriage was in pretty good shape. And it was true that compared to the struggles of some of the couples who came to us for advice, we were doing well.

It wasn't until I was forced to compare my performance as a husband to the standard of Jesus that I realized how terribly far I still had to go. I needed to be so much more gentle, more affirming, and more expressive of my feelings.

One day during a counseling session, Christine and I disagreed about something and started to argue right in front of Dan. He let us go on for a while before he began to laugh and told us, "You two are the worst fighters. You won't ever get anything resolved if you fight like that! You've both got to learn how to fight."

To begin with, Dan told me I didn't fight fair. "Guerrilla warfare," he called my style. Whenever Christine raised an issue, I'd come out blasting away. Then, while she was still reeling, I'd retreat into silence and never really engage in any discussion with her.

As a second tactic, when Christine would confront me about something, I'd respond, "You're right. I'm sorry. I'm such a jerk. I'll never be able to please you." Then Christine would feel so terrible for causing me such guilt that she'd back off and quit pressing the issue.

Whichever tactic I employed, the results were the same. We didn't ever resolve the real issues. Dan helped me see that.

It seemed he would gently but firmly challenge me with something new each session. I particularly recall the day he asked Christine, "What would be the greatest, most wonderful thing you could say about Tim, the greatest compliment you could pay him as a husband?"

She thought for a minute and then answered, "Well, I guess it would be to say, 'He's my best friend.' "

Dan turned to me and asked, "How do you feel about that?"

"I think that's good," I told him.

"Tim," Dan said, looking me in the eye, "if I were sitting in your place right now and I thought that was the highest compliment my wife could pay me as her husband, I'd be in tears."

"What do you mean?"

"A dog can be your best friend. A husband needs to be so much more—an intimate lover, a protector, a source of security and affirmation . . ."

Those words really convicted me. I knew I wanted to be all those things and more to Christine.

Christine
♥♥♥♥♥

DAN DIDN'T CONCENTRATE ALL HIS ATTENTION ON TIM. HE TOLD me I needed to work on "offering your heart to Tim."

"What do you mean?" I wanted to know.

"You're more comfortable with surface replies than you are sharing your intimate feelings with Tim. You'll say what you think needs to be done to solve a problem, but you don't tell Tim how you really feel."

He was right. "Why do I do that?" I asked.

"Why do you *think* you do that?" he answered.

"Maybe because I'm afraid to open up completely with Tim."

He nodded. "I think you may be right. And I also think you're not vulnerable with Tim anymore."

"Not vulnerable?" I responded. "I feel vulnerable to Tim. He knows everything about me. I tell him everything. We talk."

"You're transparent with Tim," Dan said, "but I don't think you're really vulnerable. There's a big difference."

I remember going home confused and wondering just what Dan meant by *vulnerable*. So I looked up the word in my dictionary: "Capable of being wounded. Open to attack." And I thought, *Of course I'm not vulnerable. I'd have to be nuts!*

I was transparent. I was willing to let Tim know everything about me. He could see me, but it was through this bulletproof glass I'd erected to protect myself.

What Dan was saying was that to be vulnerable, I needed to lower my defenses and "offer my heart." He wanted me to tell Tim exactly how I felt—respectfully, lovingly, honestly. And that was scary.

I remember the first occasion I tried to do that. We were rushing around trying to get Stephanie and Ryan ready to go to something at church when Tim got impatient and said something sharply to me. I recalled the steps Dan had advocated, so I stopped right in the middle of all that commotion and said, "Tim, when you speak harshly like that, it really hurts me."

Tim immediately got defensive. "I didn't speak sharply to you.

I'm just in a hurry. We've got to be going or we'll be late."

Trying my best to follow Dan's suggestions, I calmly said, "I understand you're in a hurry and probably didn't mean anything by it. But your words seemed harsh to me. And I just wanted you to know that when you speak to me like that, it really hurts."

However, when Tim went out the door with the kids a few minutes later, he was angry, and I thought, *This sharing my feelings stuff is never going to work. It's hopeless.*

When he returned later in the evening, however, Tim came into the kitchen and put his arms around me. "You know, you were right," he said. "I did speak harshly to you. I'm sorry. I guess I do that a lot when I'm feeling under pressure. I'll try to work on it."

I couldn't believe it. I gave him a huge hug and thanked him for listening and just acknowledging my feelings. That was real progress. And the progress continued over the next few weeks.

Tim became an approachable man. Not only did I feel more free to bring up problems, but I also found it easier to open up emotionally.

One night in bed, Tim could tell I was upset. "What's wrong?" he wanted to know.

I was afraid to say it because Tim wouldn't have heard me before, but I thought, *Offer your heart, Christine. Don't answer, "Nothing."*

"I'm so worried about Nicole," I told him. Then I poured out so much of the hurt and worry I'd kept bottled inside for months.

Instead of pulling away, getting quiet, or trying to give quick answers as he always had before, Tim just cuddled me and listened until I finished. Then he pulled my head against his shoulder and said, "I know it's hard, isn't it?"

I began to see how our new patterns of communication not only enabled us to begin resolving conflicts we'd never successfully addressed in 11 years of marriage, but they also opened up the intimacy valves in our relationship. We were beginning to talk on a whole new, wonderful level.

CHAPTER TWENTY

Decision Time

Christine
♥♥♥♥♥

OUR RELATIONSHIP FELT EXCITING, FRESH, AND INTIMATE. IT WAS AS if we fell in love all over again. We were learning to resolve conflicts, really resolve them, for the first time in our marriage. We were listening to each other. There was a new sense of passion. We both felt we were growing so much closer, so much stronger in our marriage.

But until we got to Florida in February to begin the 1993 spring training, I don't think either of us realized just how much our pattern of relating to each other had changed over the off-season. Tim was gone all day working out at the Reds' camp, so when he got home in the afternoon, he was too exhausted to do much talking.

When he arrived home one day toward the end of the first week of camp, I told him how much I missed him that day. He confessed he missed his time with me and the kids, too. We both admitted a genuine sense of sadness about facing another year in the familiar baseball grind. After getting so excited about our relationship and spending so much time growing together the previous few months, we were beginning to understand what we would have to sacrifice to continue playing baseball. We started to ask ourselves the question: *Are we willing to make that sacrifice?*

Tim even said, "Baseball seems so much more like work this year. My heart's just not in it anymore. My passion is here with you and the kids."

The next day, I was talking to Charla, a college girl from our church in Indiana who had lived with us a few weeks before coming to Florida to help take care of the children. I told her a little about our conversation, and she said, "You know, Christine,

I haven't said anything because I didn't think it was really my place. But I've noticed a real change since we've been here in Florida. Tim acts almost sad when he leaves to go to the ballpark. It seems his real passion is here at home."

"That's almost exactly what Tim said," I told her.

"Why not tell him how you really feel then?" she asked.

"Because I wouldn't want to do anything or say anything that might pressure him to leave the game he has loved all his life— even though I'd like nothing better right now than for him to retire."

"But Christine," she said, "you're his wife. If you can't tell your husband what you see and how you feel, who can?"

I thought about her words all day. I thought about what Dan had taught us in counseling, how I needed to be willing to offer my heart.

That evening, I went into our room and sat on the edge of the bed, where Tim was reading. Despite the conviction I needed to do this, I had a hard time saying what I wanted to say.

I felt guilty admitting I had needs that weren't being met. For years, I had become accustomed to not having my needs met. I hesitated to say what my heart really desired, fearing I'd be hurt by Tim's reaction.

Finally I spoke. "You know how we were talking last night about how hard it's been the past few days to sacrifice the closeness we've had and the time we've had together the past few months? How do you really feel, Tim? Do you really want to walk away from baseball? Could you actually walk away?"

Tim answered my question with a question. "How would you feel about me retiring?"

I wanted to protest and say, "I asked you first!" But instead, I decided to answer him as honestly as I could. "I'm scared," I said. "Scared we would miss the game and all the friends we have. I'm scared you'll regret the decision. I'm scared about what it would mean for our future. What would you do? Baseball is the only career you've ever had. But I'm also scared about the effect another season of baseball will have on our family and our marriage.

"How do you feel?" I asked him.

"I'm scared about leaving the game for all the reasons you mentioned," he admitted. "I know I'd miss it. I would miss our friends. And I worry about having regrets.

"But I'm also afraid of what baseball does to Stephanie and Ryan. Nicole has so many needs. I'm afraid for our marriage. I know you need my help, especially with Wayne coming in a few weeks." (We were in the process of adopting another child, a little Vietnamese boy.)

What encouraged me most was Tim's openness. He expressed his feelings with the same honesty I had. And before we fell asleep that night, he told me, "I'm going to begin praying and asking God to show me whether I should retire."

Tim

JANUARY 1 WAS USUALLY A TRIGGER FOR ME. ONCE THE COLLEGE football bowl games were over, I began to get the itch for baseball. But 1993 was different. After we packed for spring training and began the long drive to Florida, I still couldn't muster up any of the usual anticipation and excitement about reporting to camp with all the other pitchers and catchers. The feel of warm sunshine on tired muscles, the smell of fresh-cut grass, the boisterous sounds of clubhouse camaraderie—none of the traditional spring sensations aroused those familiar feelings. Even in the first few days of camp, when I realized my rigorous off-season training had paid off and I was throwing better than I had in years, I just couldn't get excited about the prospects of another baseball season.

Out on the field doing calisthenics or throwing on the mound, I would think, *What am I doing out here? I'd rather be with Christine and the kids.*

After we talked so honestly about retiring and I told Christine I would ask God for guidance, I also called a handful of people whom I respected for their spiritual sensitivity. When I told one of these advisers about my feelings and said that I wondered if something was wrong with me for feeling that way, he laughed. "You mean something must be wrong because you want to be with your wife and family?" he asked. He went on to tell me he had known many other men from business and other professions who had given up high-paying jobs and powerful positions because of their commitment to family. That reassured me.

Still, I wrestled with the decision for almost a week. Every day, the thought of retirement seemed more and more appealing. It became almost a running joke between Christine and me. Every morning she asked, "Where are you today?"

I would grin and give her an updated reading on my feelings. At first it was "about 30 percent" leaning toward retirement. The next day it was 50 percent, then 65 percent.

By the second Thursday of camp, I was up to about "90 percent certain" on the old retire-o-meter. That night, Christine stayed home with the kids while I went alone to a concert featuring contemporary Christian music artist Michael English and the group 4Him.

My drive to the concert, which took over an hour on the interstate, gave me some time to think. As I drove, I pulled out my notebook, set it on the seat beside me, and began to list the pros and cons of retirement. That made me realize my biggest reason not to retire was money. That bothered me.

Then, during the concert itself, the lyrics of one of the songs 4Him sang, "The Basics of Life," hit me right between the eyes:

> *Oh and we need the passion*
> *that burned long ago. . .*
>
> *We need to get back to*
> *the basics of life.*
> *A heart that is pure and*
> *a love that is blind*
> *A faith that is fervently*
> *Grounded in Christ*
> *The hope that endures*
> *for all time*
> *These are the basics*
> *we need to get back to*
> *the basics of life.*

When they finished that song, I knew, right there in the middle of the concert, what I wanted and needed to do.

Christine
♥♥♥♥♥

I WAS ALREADY IN BED WHEN TIM GOT HOME THAT NIGHT. BUT when he climbed under the sheets and cuddled up next to me, I was awake enough to hear him say, "I've made up my mind. I'm retiring."

"You are?" I was so shocked, I made him tell me everything about the evening.

When he told me about writing out his pros and cons list on the way to the concert, I couldn't believe it. "That's exactly what I did after you left," I told him. "I took a long walk around the lake and made my own list." We compared notes and learned we had reached the same conclusion.

Tim went on to recount the concert and the song that had hit him so hard. He concluded by saying, "I'm going to do it."

"When?" I asked.

"I think I need to wait until Saturday morning. If the Lord doesn't do something drastic to change my mind by then, I'll tell the Reds."

By Friday night, Tim knew he'd made the right decision and figured it was time to tell the kids.

Tim

I CALLED STEPHANIE AND RYAN TOGETHER AND SAT THEM SIDE BY side on the bed in Ryan's room. "I have some important news to tell you," I began. "You know how when I play baseball, I have to travel and be gone a lot?"

They nodded.

"And you don't like that?"

They shook their heads solemnly. *No, they didn't like that at all!*

"Well, you know what I'm gonna do? I'm gonna go in there tomorrow morning, and I'm gonna tell them, 'You know what? I don't want to play baseball anymore.' Ryan and Stephanie, you know why I'm gonna do that? Because I love you, and I want to be a daddy that's able to stay home more. I want to be with you more, and it hurts me to leave town. It makes me sad, too, to leave you guys. I want to be home more. So I'm gonna do this because I love you."

Christine

I SAW HUGE SMILES FROM WHERE I WAS QUIETLY WATCHING EVERY-thing. Stephanie jumped up, threw her arms around Tim's neck, and said, "Oh, thank you, Daddy. Thank you for loving me so much!"

Ryan came hopping out of his room like a bunny rabbit, shouting at me, "I have great news! Great news!"

"What news, Ryan?" I asked.

"Daddy says he's going to 'tire because he loves us! He's not going to play baseball no more."

Tim

THERE WAS NO TURNING BACK AFTER THAT, WHICH MEANT I DIDN'T sleep much on Friday night. Not that I didn't feel certain about retirement, but I realized the decision I had made was about to change my life forever.

I rose early Saturday morning, February 27, 1993. Too keyed up to consider breakfast, I dressed and drove straight from our rented Lakeland house to the Reds' spring training facility in Plant City. Walking into the clubhouse at 8:00 A.M., I hoped to catch my manager, Tony Perez, and get the whole thing over with.

But I arrived too early and had to spend a nervous few minutes scanning the morning paper, pretending everything was normal as a few players began straggling in. Finally the clubhouse manager stuck his head in the locker room and said, "Tony's here now."

I found him in an outer room, where a number of staff people were already milling around. "Can I talk to you a minute?" I asked.

"Sure," he said with a nod. "What's up?"

I glanced around the room. "In private? Could we talk in your office?"

He grabbed a cup of coffee as I followed him into his office. He closed the door and sat at his desk while I sat in a chair beside it.

"I've been struggling with something for days," I began, "and I've finally come to a decision. I've realized my heart is really with my family, and I just don't have any passion out on the ball field anymore. I've decided to retire today."

Tony set his cup down on his desk and looked as if he were about to choke on his coffee. "You what?" he asked.

I told him how I just couldn't work up any enthusiasm since spring training started. I explained that my children had special needs and that I wanted to be home for them and my wife. I couldn't do that if I continued to play baseball.

"I want you to know," Tony said, "that we were expecting your experience and leadership to be a big help for our team this year. But I can see how serious you are about this, so I won't even try to talk you out of it." He went on to tell me he respected me for what I was doing, and he wished me luck in the future. Then he walked with me over to the general manager's office to tell him the news.

The GM was out, so I went back into the clubhouse to wait again. While I was talking to the pitching coach on one side of the locker room, I saw my old friend Jeff Reardon, who also had signed with the Reds over the winter, come in and walk to his locker. I went over and sat down beside him on a bench.

"Don't tell me," he said before I got out one word. "You don't have to. You're retiring, aren't you?"

During the first days of camp, we had honestly discussed the demands baseball placed on our families. He knew me well enough to see what was coming.

"I don't know if I could do what you're doing," he said, "but

I wish you and Christine the best."

I told Jeff how much I appreciated his friendship and how much he had meant to me early in my career with the Expos. I thanked him, and we said our good-byes.

Reds general manager Jim Bowden was also very understanding. I was in his office for only a couple of minutes.

Then came the emotional task of cleaning out my locker, realizing I would never again be at home in a major-league clubhouse. Since I started playing Little League at the age of eight and for the last 25 years, the game of baseball had been a major part of my life. It shaped my everyday existence, influenced my decisions, and provided me with an identity. For my entire adult life, I had been Tim Burke, professional baseball player.

All that was about to change.

When I had stuffed the last of my personal belongings into my Cincinnati Reds equipment bag, I headed out of the locker room door to meet the waiting reporters. They asked why I was retiring. That's when I said, "Baseball is going to do just fine without me. It's not going to miss a beat. But I'm the only father my children have. I'm the only husband my wife has. And they need me a lot worse than baseball does."

Then it was out the door, tossing my equipment into the car and getting away as quickly as I could.

But I couldn't escape a feeling of grief and loss, as if I'd just experienced the death of a lifelong friend I would never see again. A consuming sadness welled up from deep inside, and I had to wipe away the tears as I drove off, looking back in my rearview mirror at the Reds' spring training stadium growing smaller and smaller in the distance.

CHAPTER TWENTY-ONE

A Brand-New Game

Christine
♥♥♥♥♥

THAT FIRST DAY OF RETIREMENT WAS GREAT. WHEN TIM RETURNED from the ballpark after officially informing the Reds, the kids and I surprised him. We welcomed him home with a front porch full of balloons, candy, and little teddy bears, each with a personal little "thank you" note from all of us.

"Well, Daddy did it!" Tim announced in greeting. "No more baseball for me."

The kids cheered. But I couldn't help sensing some of Tim's sadness.

"How would you all like to go swimming?" Tim asked after appreciating our surprises and reading our notes. Stephanie and Ryan cheered again. The house we rented had a pool, so we all went outside where, for the next two hours, Tim splashed and played in the water with the kids.

At one point Ryan asked, "Can we do this every day, Daddy?"

"We'll do lots of things, Ryan," Tim answered with a laugh.

We spent the entire day in a celebration with the kids, simply enjoying one another's company. That evening, we went out to eat with good friends who had come to Florida to see Tim pitch in spring training but ended up sharing our little retirement dinner instead.

The next morning, we slept in late. I was awakened by Tim cuddling up close, gently kissing me on the ear and whispering, "I'm still here. I don't have to go to the ballpark today." I thought, *Mmm, I could sure get used to this.*

We talked a lot those first few days, trying to recapture some of the intimacy we felt before we started spring training. We began to realize that after 12 years of professional baseball, we suddenly had a freedom we had never known before. We could make choices about what to do, where, and when. For the first time in our marriage, we had time for *us*.

Our last week in Florida, we asked our baby-sitter to take care of the kids for five hours every day while Tim and I went out by the lake to be alone. It was like our own personal marriage retreat. We began to take everything Dan had taught us in counseling and try to apply it to 11 years of marriage.

I bought each of us a notebook to use as a journal, and we spent most of the first day writing our answers to one basic question: What things have hurt you the most but you've been too afraid to say so? We vowed we would be completely honest with each other. As we revealed our lists, we agreed not to respond to any charges, not to try to defend ourselves—just to listen and milk out all the hurt. Our intention was to excavate all the junk and debris we had buried and never dealt with in our marriage so that we could lay a new, solid foundation for the rest of our lives.

We spent one whole day on the theme of forgiveness. And the final day, we wrote out and discussed goals for our new life together and talked about what boundaries we needed to set to protect our marriage and family priorities.

We knew baseball was behind us, but we determined not to let whatever came next interfere with the priorities we set.

What surprised us the most was the difference between our hearts' priorities and our everyday actions. In our hearts, we agreed that our own relationships with God needed highest priority, then our marriage, our children, and whatever ministry God opened up for us. But when we honestly examined our lives, we realized we too often made the kids our top priority, we bumped God down to second place, and we often placed ministry opportunities above even our own relationship.

We determined together to get our priorities into proper order and keep them there.

All in all, we had an incredible week together. Because of the communication skills we learned during counseling over the winter, we were able to talk about issues we never even acknowledged before. It was, without a doubt, the single most important week in our entire marriage.

Tim

IT ELEVATED US TO A WHOLE NEW LEVEL IN OUR RELATIONSHIP IN terms of how we felt, as well as how we communicated. We moved back to Indiana at the end of that time, feeling ready to face together whatever the future held.

While I obviously considered my decision to retire a personal milestone, I didn't expect anyone else to notice. I figured my name would show up the next day on one line in a few newspapers, in fine print in the transactions report: "Retired: Cincinnati Reds pitcher Tim Burke." Then I would be completely forgotten.

Neither Christine nor I could believe it when we arrived at our house in Indiana to discover a dozen or more messages on our answering machine from national media, including newspaper and magazine reporters, "Good Morning, America," "Entertainment Tonight," and even "The Tonight Show."

What do they want with us? I wondered.

It seems we had become a national human-interest story. Evidently our jaded world is so hungry for good news that the media decided everyone should hear the simple story of a baseball pitcher who retired so he could be with his family. Because we realized it gave us a platform from which we could promote adoption and talk about the importance of family, we cooperated with most of the interview requests.

Amazing. Barely a week after I retired from baseball, I was getting more attention for trying to be a good husband and father than I ever received as a professional athlete.

Christine
♥♥♥♥♥

SO MUCH HAPPENED SO QUICKLY THAT I DON'T THINK THE SIGNIFicance of Tim's retirement really began to sink in for several weeks. But I remember when it did.

Tim was gone one day when we got a package in the mail

containing cassette tapes of an interview Tim and I did with Dr. James Dobson for his daily "Focus on the Family" radio program. We talked about Tim's retirement, our children, and our new commitment to family. The programs hadn't aired yet, and I was eager to listen to the interview, so I took the tapes with me in the car as I ran errands that afternoon.

Listening to the interview, it was as if my own voice and my own responses to Dr. Dobson's questions faded into the background. I really didn't hear Dr. Dobson's words, either. What I focused on that day was the familiar but somehow larger-than-life sound of my husband's voice. As he talked about the difficulty of his decision to give up baseball—the game he had loved and played all his life—I think I realized for the first time what that decision truly cost him. He hadn't just given up a game; he had given up a life and a career he loved. He had said good-bye forever to a lifelong friend and walked away from the one big, central dream he had pursued since boyhood.

I heard Tim's voice, loud and penetrating, over the car stereo: "Christine has had to be mother, father, doctor, mover, plumber, traveling secretary, and so many other things in our family for so long. . . . This was the perfect way to show her how much I love her."

At that point, I pulled the car into a parking place, leaned my head against the steering wheel, and wept. I could accept the fact that Tim had retired for the children, and I had freely expressed my gratitude to God as well as Tim for his love and commitment as a father. But what struck me full force for the first time now was that he had done it for me, Christine. Not just the children. For *me*.

I realized I didn't know how to respond to, or even accept, that kind of attention and sacrificial love. My father left before I was born; I never knew a father's unconditional love. The men I encountered growing up certainly didn't love me that way. No experience in my life prepared me to deal with that kind of love. I prayed that God would somehow help me find a way to accept that love and show Tim how grateful I was for what he had done—for me. I could almost see the headline in the morning paper: "Woman dies of too much love."

I felt so blessed.

Tim

MANY PEOPLE HAVE A HARD TIME UNDERSTANDING HOW I COULD walk away from all the acclaim and the money that are such a part of major-league baseball. I hope this book helps explain it.

We tried never to live extravagantly when I made a lot of money in baseball, and we invested prudently, so that made leaving easier. But there remains a lot of uncertainty about our future. We don't yet know how or even exactly where the Lord would like us to spend the rest of our lives. We don't know what's ahead for our family or our children. We don't even know how many children we may eventually have in our family, since we're not finished adopting.

But we're finally able to live with that kind of uncertainty because the experiences Christine and I have shared in our adventure together have taught us one overriding truth: We can trust God if we just let Him have control.

As I face this new stage in our lives, I've been especially encouraged by a couple of promises God made to His people in the Old Testament. Jeremiah 29:11 says, " 'I know the plans I have for you,' declares the LORD, 'plans to prosper you and not to harm you, plans to give you hope and a future.' "

And Joshua 1:8 says, "Do not let this Book of the Law depart from your mouth; meditate on it day and night, so that you may be careful to do everything written in it. Then you will be prosperous and successful."

What those verses tell me is that if we will just continue to obey God, He will, indeed, prosper us. Maybe we won't prosper by the world's standards. I don't expect to ever again make the kind of money I made playing baseball. I don't expect the kind of attention and acclaim I received as a major-league pitcher. God's idea of prosperity for us goes much deeper than money or fame; He wants to prosper us in our relationships—in our families, with others, and ultimately in our relationship with Him.

That is why this past Thanksgiving, when I sat down to make a list of the ways God had blessed me, I came up with what may seem like a strange list. Among the things I'm thankful for are a bad marriage; infertility; my drinking problem; Christine's broken neck; the end of my baseball career; and four special-needs children, including a brain-damaged, one-handed little girl who may or may not ever be potty-trained, say "I love you," or call me Daddy.

I can honestly say I'm thankful for those things because each of them has played an important role in drawing me closer to the Lord.

Nicole is a wonderful example because she has taught me so much. She has become so attached to me, clinging to me with all her might when I hold her, throwing her arms wide in loving, joyous welcome whenever she sees me across the room. She loves with such a pure and unconditional love that it challenges and convicts me every day. She's like an angel in the midst of our family, modeling the perfect and abundant love of God.

Not that it isn't difficult and heartbreaking to see the way she has suffered and still suffers. But even her limitations recently taught me an important lesson.

One morning, driving to meet a friend for breakfast, I was feeling especially frustrated. I was praying, telling God how upset I was with Nicole's inability to understand just how much I love her and how much she means to me. I have such strong feelings for her, but I can't express them in a way that she can comprehend.

Then God spoke to my heart. He said, "Tim, that's how I feel about you. You won't let Me show you fully how much I love you and care about you. You mean more to Me than even Nicole means to you! Nicole can't help it that she can't let you in, but you can choose to let Me in!"

Christine

I GOT A LETTER FROM A HURTING MOTHER ONE DAY. SHE, TOO, HAD a very sick child, and like mine, her heart was heavy and almost breaking. She had heard the broadcast of our interview with Dr. Dobson and was writing to ask, "How do you make it through a tragedy like you've had with your child without losing your mind and falling apart completely?"

I wrote her back, "Unfortunately, there are no easy answers. No quick fixes." I told her that the only solution I'd found was not an easy one.

From Nicole's tragedy, I've learned that I have two options. The first is to spend the rest of my life demanding that God answer my "Why?" questions—trying to figure it all out. But in doing that, I would be pulling away from God and searching for comfort in my own understanding. Years ago, that's how I always handled trials, but I had ended up hardened and isolated.

The second option was to tell God exactly how I felt, to wrestle with Him like the psalmist David. I could ask "Why?" but if I didn't get an answer, I could still say, "I don't understand this at all, God, but I'm going to trust You anyway."

I chose the second option, which is hard for someone like me with a long history of distrust, who has made a lifelong habit of building walls of self-protection, always looking for ways to maintain control. But I'm slowly learning that only when I'm willing to let down the walls, expose my weakness, and trust God enough to let Him control what I don't understand and can't change myself—only then can I be truly strong.

Recently, He asked me to do just that again. This time it concerned our newest son, Wayne. When he arrived from Vietnam, we thought, *This shouldn't be too hard.* All he had was a club-foot. One or two surgeries and he'd be up and running just like all the other children. But what we thought would be easy turned out to be a nightmare.

That first week when Wayne came home, we took him to the hospital to have the usual blood tests done. Our doctor left the orders at the lab, and the testing quickly began. It was a long, hard day for Wayne. Late that afternoon, we went back to get the test results. The nurse told us we needed to call our doctor as soon as possible. She handed Tim the receiver and dialed the number for him.

I sat on the couch with Wayne and strained to hear what Tim was saying. "He has what?" Tim questioned. "What do you do for that?" He then turned his back to me so I couldn't hear.

My heart was racing as I thought, *What's wrong?*

Tim hung up the phone, shaking his head in despair.

"What was that all about?" I asked.

"I'm afraid Wayne has hepatitis B," he told me.

"Well, what does that mean? What is hepatitis B?"

"It's a liver disease that's very contagious."

"Contagious!" I screamed. "How contagious?"

"If we're not careful, we could get it. We might already have contracted it."

"You mean the other children . . ." With that, I started crying. "What do we have to do?"

Tim frowned as he answered, "I'm afraid there's not much they can do. The doctor even said Wayne is at high risk for liver cancer when he gets older. He also said hepatitis B carriers shouldn't be close to heart patients."

I gasped out, "Nicole's a heart patient!"

"I know, Honey, I know."

We both looked down at Wayne, who was smiling, oblivious to any of this.

Tim helped me up as he said, "Come on, Honey, let's go. The doctor said we have to bring the other children here right away for blood tests to make sure they haven't contracted the disease yet. Then we need to begin a series of shots to vaccinate them."

Stunned, I walked to the car. As soon as we got home, Tim hurried each child into the van as I sat at the kitchen table in shock. The last one he carried to the van was Nicole. When she passed by, my heart sank as I remembered what Tim had said.

The next week was long and hard. I was trying to figure all this out. Had God made His first mistake by putting a child with this disease in our home? I kept pleading with God for an answer, but He remained silent. I kept wrestling, but He said nothing. Finally I gave in and said, "Lord, I don't understand all this, but I'm going to just trust that You know what You're doing."

Right then, the Spirit of God spoke to my heart and said, "Christine, how much do you love Me?"

Quietly I answered, "You know, Lord, that I love you very much."

Then He said, "Feed My little sheep, Wayne."

Again He asked, "How much do you love Me?"

And again I answered, "Oh, Lord, I love You very much."
"Then feed this little sheep."

A third time, just as He did with Peter in the Bible, He asked, "How much do you really love Me, Christine? Enough to love this little sheep with all your heart?"

With that, I began to weep, admitting to myself that I had been holding back from really loving Wayne. I was afraid of his disease. But I promised God, "I will take good care of this little one."

I walked into the kitchen, where Wayne was sitting in his high chair, eating breakfast. I leaned over and, for the first time since hearing of his disease, kissed him and said, "I love you."

Tim

MY RETIREMENT COULDN'T HAVE COME AT A MORE OPPORTUNE time. My special-needs family suddenly became even needier. I marvel at God's timing. We had over 30 trips to the doctor this last summer. It was a pleasure for me to take over as daddy the driver. I sat with each child through each doctor visit and truly loved it. For the first time as a father and husband, I felt I could really help my family.

Also, for the first time in 11 years, Christine and I got to work through a heartbreak together. We didn't have to grieve Wayne's disease separately. We grieved it side by side.

But we also rejoiced together. About the time we began thinking about this book, Nicole's seizures suddenly stopped. What a blessed relief! Why did they stop? Will they ever come back? The doctors can't tell us. We don't know. What I do know is that our family life suddenly became a lot less stressful. So much so that we're considering a fifth adoption before long.

Christine

OUR DESIRE, AFTER ALL IS SAID AND DONE, IS THAT ONE PART OF OUR story will stand tall above the rest. Namely, we want you to realize that if it were not for Jesus, there would be no Tim and Christine Burke marriage filled with love or a future full of hope. Nor would there be any delightful pictures in a photo album of a darling boy from Vietnam, two precious girls from Korea, and a wonderful boy from Guatemala. There would simply be no story to tell if not for Him. He took something broken down and nearly destroyed and slowly made it fresh and new, giving it hope again.

Tim

SINCE I RETIRED FROM BASEBALL, I'VE HAD MANY PEOPLE TELL ME, "That's fine for you, but I can't quit my job. I have to support my family." Some men have even told me that my story made them feel guilty for not giving up their jobs for their families.

Because of that, I want to make it clear that I'm *not* saying all men ought to give up their careers or stay home with their families all the time. I realize few are in a position to do what I did. And even those who could shouldn't necessarily do it.

What I am saying is this: All of us need to do a serious evaluation of our outward priorities. I say *outward* because I think that for years, in my heart, I believed in the importance of putting God first, Christine second, our children third, and my work fourth. But that wasn't how I was living.

For me, getting my outward priorities into proper alignment required my retirement from baseball. But I've since talked to other men who rearranged their priorities by rescheduling work travel to spend an extra day a week at home. Another man told me he had begun taking work home so he could spend more time with and around his family. So there are many ways to address work versus family priorities.

Of course, work isn't the only thing that can foul up our priorities. I find I still have to be careful with my leisure-time interests. I'm a big hockey and football fan, I love going to concerts, and I enjoy playing golf. Now that I have more time to pursue those interests, I have to remember not to let them take precedence over my time with God, my wife, and my family.

All in all, adjusting to life after baseball has been much easier than I expected. I've always been the kind of person who set goals and then worked toward them. So I simply changed my goals.

All my life, I dreamed of being a major-league pitcher. For eight wonderful seasons, I fulfilled that dream.

Now I have a bigger dream. I want to be a major-league husband and a major-league dad.

"A Place for You"

Tim

EARLIER IN THE BOOK, I MENTIONED A SPECIAL FRIEND NAMED Wayne Watson. Wayne has been with me through many highs and lows. He was there the day I was selected to the All-Star team (he lives in Houston). He was also there the night before Nicole's open-heart surgery, quietly comforting me with his presence.

In a lot of ways, Wayne has been the brother I lost. (God has a way of providing exactly what you need when you need it most.) Wayne and his wife, Lynn, along with countless others, have supported us in each adoption. That has meant more to us than words can say. Wayne, who is a superb singer/songwriter, wrote the following song partially about our family. But ultimately, it's a song that pertains to each and every one of us.

A Place for You

One little stranger—one in a million
One homeless angel—one helpless child
In the fields that God has sown
Blessings live, life is grown
An empty space, the Father knew
There is a place for you

So come cross the ocean— safe to the harbor
Into a family two worlds away
Far from your tragedy—safe and secure
All along the Father knew
There is a place for you

Every child in God's family—souls orphaned
   at birth
Knows a hunger, a thirst to be wanted
But every son, every daughter
Whether pauper or king
Can celebrate heaven's welcoming arms

Stand with me children—come out from
   the shadows
Room for so many, His promise is true
It's a common ground—every soul
Wants to live and be loved
And in the sight of heaven's view
There is a place for you

To learn about *spiritual* adoption, please turn to the next page.

Adoption was easy for Christine, but I struggled with it. More than that, at first I outright resisted it. I did not want to make such a commitment and change of life-style. Gradually, however, the Lord changed my heart, and I chose to make a commitment to children.

The same was true of my spiritual adoption. At first I resisted, not wanting such a commitment. However, in time and with careful study and a change of heart, I became a Christian along with Christine.

For the first time in our lives, we were beginning to understand what spiritual adoption meant. How marvelous it was that Jesus' death on the cross wasn't for a select few. Rather, it was for all, regardless of status, race, or creed. Listen to how the Bible says it:

> If you confess with your mouth, "Jesus is Lord," and believe in your heart that God raised him from the dead, you will be saved. For it is with your heart that you believe and are justified, and it is with your mouth that you confess and are saved. As the Scripture says, "Anyone who trusts in him will never be put to shame." For there is no difference between Jew and Gentile—the same Lord is the Lord of all and richly blesses all who call on him, for, "Everyone who calls on the name of the Lord will be saved." (Romans 10:9-13)

Maybe you want to "call on the name of the Lord," but you're not sure how to do that. Well, we've found a wonderful diagram that shows you how near you are to taking that final "step." It illustrates the five stages of the human heart.

What Step Are You On?*

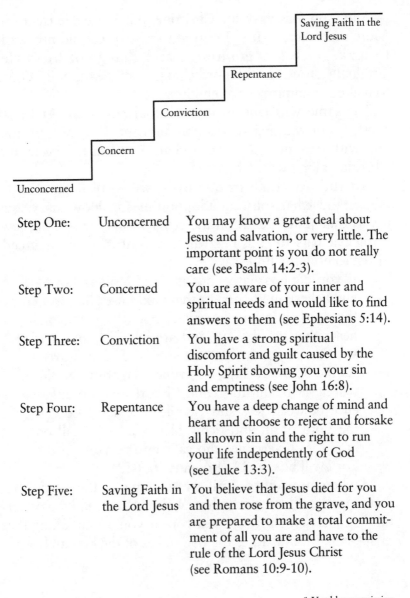

Saving Faith in the
Lord Jesus

Repentance

Conviction

Concern

Unconcerned

Step One: Unconcerned   You may know a great deal about
                              Jesus and salvation, or very little. The
                              important point is you do not really
                              care (see Psalm 14:2-3).

Step Two: Concerned   You are aware of your inner and
                              spiritual needs and would like to find
                              answers to them (see Ephesians 5:14).

Step Three: Conviction   You have a strong spiritual
                              discomfort and guilt caused by the
                              Holy Spirit showing you your sin
                              and emptiness (see John 16:8).

Step Four: Repentance   You have a deep change of mind and
                              heart and choose to reject and forsake
                              all known sin and the right to run
                              your life independently of God
                              (see Luke 13:3).

Step Five: Saving Faith in You believe that Jesus died for you
              the Lord Jesus   and then rose from the grave, and you
                              are prepared to make a total commit-
                              ment of all you are and have to the
                              rule of the Lord Jesus Christ
                              (see Romans 10:9-10).

* Used by permission.

When you make a saving commitment to Jesus (step five), the heavenly Father adopts you into His family as He forgives *all* of your sin.

God loves you and has provided a way for you to be reconciled to Him for *eternity*. He provided the forgiveness; He wants us to respond with repentance and commitment (see 2 Peter 3:9).

You may be unsure about how to pray and tell God this. To help, we wrote a simple prayer that you can repeat:

"Dear God, I admit that I have sinned and need to be forgiven. I believe in Jesus and that He died on the cross to forgive all of my sin. I am willing to repent of my sin and, with Your help, live a life that would be pleasing to You. I surrender doing things my way and choose to do them the way you've asked me to in the Bible. Right now I do as Scripture has said: I call on You, Lord, to forgive me and save me. Thank You for taking me just as I am into Your family. In Jesus' name, amen."

It's our prayer that your journey would be healing and life-changing! We pray that the Lord will help you grow as you study the Scriptures. We also pray that you'll sense the awesome and abundant love that He has for *you!*

Remember what Wayne Watson's song said . . . "There is a place for you."

If you would like more material on this, please write for a free *full* copy of the tract we used, "Step Up to Life": Step Up to Life Press, 15555 West Dodge Road, Omaha, NE 68154.

(Thank you, Pastor Murdoch, for your help in explaining the gospel message.)

Adoption Information

Holt International Children's Services

We highly recommend Holt International. This agency is the one we've worked with for all four of our children. Here is how they describe themselves:

"Holt International Children's Services of Eugene, Oregon, provides a wide range of programs for homeless children overseas. Because some children cannot be placed with permanent families in their birth countries, Holt is always seeking adoptive families all across the United States. Holt needs families who wish to love and parent children from Asia, Latin America, and Eastern Europe. These children range from healthy infants to teenagers. Some children have disabilities, and some are sibling groups. Holt's motto—'Every child deserves a home of his own'—is based on a Christian conviction that children need and deserve the security, belonging, and nurturing of parents, and that the love of parents can transcend the barriers of race and nationality. Holt also has sponsorship programs that enable donors to help provide care and support for children who need families."

You can contact Holt International at 1195 City View, Eugene, OR 97402; (503) 687-2202.

Adoptive Families of America (AFA)

AFA is a private, nonprofit organization that seeks to create opportunities for successful adoptive placement. It is not an adoption agency but a referral service that can direct you to the agency nearest you. It has a list of 300 different agencies across the United States, and you can also write or call for a free general information packet. Contact AFA at 3333 Highway 100 N, Minneapolis, MN 55422; (612) 535-4829.

Recommended Reading

Most of the books listed below can be found in any Christian bookstore. For the one exception, we've provided a mailing address.

On parenting
Pat Holt and Grace Ketterman, *When You Feel Like Screaming* (Harold Shaw).
James Dobson, *The Strong-Willed Child* (Tyndale).
James Dobson, *Hide or Seek* (Baker).
James Dobson, *The New Dare to Discipline* (Tyndale).
Gary Smalley and John Trent, *The Blessing* (Thomas Nelson).
H. Norman Wright, *The Power of a Parent's Words* (Regal).

On self-esteem
Josh McDowell, *His Image, My Image* (Here's Life).
Robert McGee, *Search for Significance* (Rapha Publishing).

On marriage
Jimmy Evans, *Marriage on the Rock* (Vincom, Inc., P.O. Box 702400, Tulsa, OK 74170).

From Tim
Steve Farrar, *Point Man* (Multnomah/Questar).
Max Lucado, all his books (various publishers).
R. Kent Hughes, *Disciplines of a Godly Man* (Crossway).
Gary Smalley and John Trent, *The Hidden Value of a Man* (Focus on the Family).
Brennan Manning, *The Ragamuffin Gospel* (Multnomah).

From Christine
Dan Allender, *The Wounded Heart* (NavPress).
Robert E. Fisher, *Quick to Listen, Slow to Speak* (Tyndale).
Floyd McClung, Jr., *The Father Heart of God* (Harvest House).
James Dobson, *When God Doesn't Make Sense* (Tyndale).

Acknowledgments

To our precious families, thank you for loving and supporting us. We wouldn't have made it through all the rough times without you. We love and appreciate you more than you know! We are truly grateful for all the sacrifices you've made and all the patience and understanding you've given us.

To our faithful friends, thank you as well. Your loyalty and friendship have equipped us to face the challenges God has put before us. Many times, you've been there as God's hands, holding us. Other times, you've been His mouthpiece, spurring us on. We want you to know how much we love and need you!

Finally, thank you, Gregg Lewis and the Focus on the Family publishing staff, for helping us to tell our story.

A BEAUTIFUL PLACE

Wayne Watson

If you were touched by the words of the song **"A Place for You,"** quoted in **Major League Dad**, read on! You'll want to find out more about the Burkes' friend Wayne Watson.

Watson has a recent album entitled **A Beautiful Place**. This release features **"A Place for You,"** as well as the songs **"A Beautiful Place," "Walk in the Dark," "Hard Times,"** and **"A Season in Your Path."**

This recording sparkles with the wonder, mystery, and passionate conviction that embody the mercy and hope of Christ.

Visit your favorite bookstore for a cassette or CD.